favorite family dinners

Editor: Jessica Saari
Contributing Designer: Waterbury Publications, Inc., Chad Jewell

Meredith Books
1716 Locust Street
Des Moines, Iowa 50309-3023
meredithbooks.com

First Edition.

Printed in the United States of America.
ISBN: 978-0-696-24302-8

Table of Contents

Dear Sam's Club members:

This one's for you!

We set out to create an exclusive collection of dishes just for you, and the result is a compilation of irresistible recipes and beautiful photos that are perfect for any occasion. We are delighted to offer you this value-packed book at an extraordinary price.

Quality family time spent around a dinner table is extremely important. In an effort to serve you the best, Sam's Club partnered with Better Homes and Gardens® to bring you these wonderful meals. All the recipes in this book were selected because they're perfect for those hectic weeknights when time is at a premium—each is quick, easy, and most importantly, wholesome and delicious. Each meal uses money-saving products and ingredients from Sam's Club; plus, if you run out of time, you can prepare a main dish from this book and supplement it with a fabulous prepared side dish from your local Club.

Additionally, several celebrity chefs contributed their tips to help you accomplish your ideal meal. Finally, we included a chapter of contemporary recipes that speak directly to today's cooks: recipes designed to be simple, utterly impressive, and delicious while still being family-friendly.

This cookbook will help you provide it all—easily prepared delicious food that everyone in the family will love!

From our hearts to yours—Enjoy!

Sam's Club

1 Chef's Special

Check out what some of the hottest chefs are making in their kitchens these days. Tyler Florence, Sandra Lee, Rocco DiSpirito, the Deen Brothers, G. Garvin, and George Duran dish up their favorite eats.

This recipe was excerpted from Tyler Florence's cookbook Dinner at My Place.

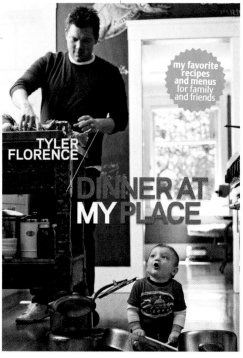

Penne with Spicy Italian Sausage, Cream, Tomatoes & Peas

START TO FINISH: 55 minutes   **MAKES:** 4 to 6 servings

- 4 links spicy Italian sausage
- 1 pound dried penne
   Extra-virgin olive oil
- 1 medium onion, chopped
- 4 garlic cloves, peeled and chopped
- 1 28-ounce can crushed San Marzano tomatoes
- ¼ cup torn fresh basil leaves
   Kosher salt and freshly ground black pepper
- 1 cup heavy whipping cream
- 2 cups peas, blanched*
- ½ cup grated Parmigiano-Reggiano, plus more for serving
   Fresh basil leaves, for garnish

1. Preheat oven to 350°F. Place the sausages in a roasting pan and roast in the preheated oven for 12 to 15 minutes, until slightly golden and just cooked. Cut sausage at an angle into bite-size pieces.

2. Place a large pot of salted water over high heat and bring to a boil. Drop the pasta into the boiling water and cook until tender yet firm (al dente).

3. Set a large, heavy-based pot over medium heat and add a 2-count of olive oil (about 2 tablespoons). Add onion and garlic and sauté until translucent and fragrant. Add tomatoes and basil; season with salt and pepper. Simmer for 15 minutes, then fold in cream and continue to simmer until rich and creamy. Add sausage, blanched peas, and Parmigiano-Reggiano. Fold together and cook for 2 to 3 minutes to allow the flavors to come together. Serve topped with a shower of cheese and garnish with basil.

*TIP: To blanch the peas, submerge them into boiling water for 2½ minutes (1 minute for frozen peas), then strain them and plunge them into ice water to stop the cooking process. Strain them again and set aside.

This recipe was excerpted from Tyler Florence's cookbook Stirring the Pot.

Grilled Cheese (Smoked Mozzarella & Basil Pesto)

START TO FINISH: 30 minutes   MAKES: 2 servings

Basil Pesto
2 cups fresh basil leaves
1 cup fresh Italian flat-leaf parsley leaves
½ cup grated Parmigiano-Reggiano
½ cup pine nuts, toasted
3 garlic cloves, peeled and roughly chopped
¼ teaspoon kosher salt
½ cup extra-virgin olive oil

Grilled Cheese Sandwiches
4 slices white sandwich bread
4 thick-cut slices smoked mozzarella
   Freshly ground black pepper
2 tablespoons unsalted butter
1 garlic clove, peeled

1. For the Basil Pesto, in a food processor combine basil, parsley, Parmigiano-Reggiano, pine nuts, garlic, salt, and oil and pulse until well combined but still rough in texture.

2. Assemble sandwiches by smearing one side of each bread slice with pesto. Layer the mozzarella slices over the pesto on half of the bread slices. Season with a few turns of freshly ground black pepper. Place the remaining bread slices, pesto sides down, over cheese to make the sandwiches.

3. In large sauté pan melt butter over medium heat. Add sandwiches and cook 2 to 3 minutes per side, until golden brown and crispy. Remove from pan and rub toasted bread with the garlic clove.

13

Turkey Meatballs

PREP: 15 minutes **COOK:** 3 to 4 hours (High) or 8 to 9 hours (Low)
MAKES: 6 servings

- 1½ pounds ground turkey
- 1¼ cups Italian bread crumbs
- ¼ cup minced onion
- 1 teaspoon bottled minced garlic
- ¼ cup chopped fresh parsley
- 1 egg, lightly beaten
  Salt and ground black pepper
- 1 jar (26-ounce) marinara sauce
- 2 cans (14.5 ounces each) diced tomatoes with basil, garlic, and oregano
- 2 teaspoons dried basil

1. In a medium bowl, combine ground turkey, bread crumbs, onion, garlic, parsley, egg, salt and pepper. With your hands, blend ingredients together and form approximately thirty 1-inch meatballs.

2. Stir together marinara sauce, tomatoes, and dried basil. Pour half of sauce mixture into a 4- to 5-quart slow cooker. Add meatballs and top with remaining sauce. Cover and cook on high heat setting for 3 to 4 hours or low heat setting for 8 to 9 hours.

Turkey Meatballs was excerpted from Semi-Homemade Fast-Fix Family Favorites

Down-Home Pot Roast

PREP: 20 minutes **MARINATE:** 4 hours **BAKE:** 3 hours
STAND 5 minutes **MAKES:** 12 servings

- 6 pounds beef chuck roast
- 2 cups red wine
- 1 cup olive oil and vinegar salad dressing
- 2 tablespoons Worcestershire sauce
- 1 envelope (0.6-ounce) zesty Italian salad dressing mix
- 2 tablespoons canola oil
- 2 brown or yellow onions, sliced
- 3 stalks celery, cut into 2-inch pieces
- 4 cups lower-sodium beef broth
- 2 packets (1.5 ounces each) meat loaf seasoning mix
- 3 pounds baby Yukon gold or fingerling potatoes, cut in half
- 1 pound baby carrots
  Celery leaves (optional)

1. Place meat in a large zip-top plastic bag. In a medium bowl, whisk together wine, olive oil and vinegar salad dressing, Worcestershire sauce, and dry Italian salad dressing mix. Pour over meat in bag. Seal bag; turn to coat meat. Marinate in refrigerator for 4 hours to overnight, turning bag occasionally.

2. Preheat oven to 325 degrees F. Remove meat from marinade and pat dry with paper towels. Discard marinade. In a large skillet, heat oil over medium heat. Add meat and brown on all sides. Place in roasting pan and set aside.

3. Add onion and celery to same skillet; cook for 3 minutes. Stir in broth and meat loaf seasoning; bring to a boil. Remove from heat and carefully pour over meat. Cover tightly with aluminum foil. Bake for 2 hours.

4. Remove roast from oven and add potatoes and carrots. Re-cover pan. Bake for 1 hour more. Remove roast, potatoes, and carrots from pan. Let meat stand for 5 minutes before slicing. Strain pan juices and set aside. Slice meat against the grain. Serve meat with potatoes, carrots, and strained pan juices. Garnish with celery leaves (optional).

Down-Home Pot Roast was excerpted from Semi-Homemade Money Saving Meals.

This recipe was excerpted from Sandra Lee's cookbook, Semi-Homemade Desserts 2.

Pink Party Cake

PREP: 25 minutes   **BAKE:** 28 minutes
CHILL: 20 minutes   **MAKES:** 10 servings

    Nonstick spray for baking
 1 package (18.25-ounce) strawberry cake mix
 1¼ cups strawberry nectar
 ⅓ cup vegetable oil
 3 eggs
 1 teaspoon almond extract
 2 drops red food coloring
 1 bar (4-ounce) white baking bar, chopped
 2 tablespoons whipping cream
 1½ cans (12 ounces each) whipped fluffy white frosting
 1 cup pink candy coating*

1. Preheat oven to 350 degrees F. Spray two 8-inch round cake pans with nonstick spray and set aside.

2. In a large bowl, combine cake mix, strawberry nectar, oil, eggs, almond extract, and red food coloring; beat with an electric mixer on low speed for 30 seconds. Scrape down sides of the bowl and beat on medium speed for 2 minutes. Pour batter into prepared cake pans.

3. Bake in preheated oven for 28 to 32 minutes or until wooden pick inserted in centers comes out clean. Cool cakes in pans on wire racks for 10 minutes. Remove cake layers from pans; cool completely on wire racks.

4. For frosting, place chopped white baking bar in a medium bowl; set aside. In a small microwave-safe bowl, microwave cream on high setting (100 percent power) for 30 seconds. Pour over baking bar and stir until smooth. Stir in frosting. Place a cake layer on a serving plate. Spread with some of the frosting and top with the remaining cake layer. Frost cake with the remaining frosting.

5. Line a 5½-inch glass bowl with foil and set aside. Place candy coating in a small microwave-safe bowl; microwave on medium setting (50 percent power) for 1½ minutes, stirring every 30 seconds. Pour melted candy coating into foil-lined bowl and chill in refrigerator about 20 minutes or until hard.

6. Lift candy coating from bowl and peel off foil. Turn candy coating over and pull a vegetable peeler along outside edge to make large curls. Arrange pink curls on top of frosted cake.

*NOTE: Candy coating is available at cake decorating supply stores. If you can't find it, substitute the same amount of chopped vanilla bark. Melt as directed; stir in 1 to 2 drops of red food coloring to make the bark pink. Continue as directed.

17

Shrimp Au Poivre with Broiled Zucchini

START TO FINISH: 20 minutes   **MAKES:** 4 servings

3   large zucchini, sliced in half horizontally and sliced into half moons
2   tablespoons extra-virgin olive oil
     Salt and freshly ground pepper
4   tablespoons unsalted butter
¼   cup fresh coarsely ground black pepper
1¼ pounds raw shrimp, peeled and deveined
1   bunch scallions, sliced thin on a bias
1   10-ounce jar spicy red pepper jelly (such as Tabasco)
½   cup pineapple juice

1. Preheat broiler on high. Line a rimmed baking sheet with foil. Toss the zucchini with olive oil and salt and pepper to taste. Spread out in a single layer on the prepared baking sheet. Broil, stirring and turning occasionally, until lightly charred and tender, about 6 minutes.

2. Meanwhile, in a large sauté pan or cast-iron skillet, heat butter over medium heat. Season shrimp with salt and dredge one side in the coarsely ground black pepper. When butter is hot and foamy, add shrimp to the pan. Cook until just cooked through, about 2 minutes per side.

3. Remove shrimp from pan and add scallions. Cook, stirring occasionally, for about 2 minutes. Add red pepper jelly and pineapple juice and bring to a boil. Cook until sauce is slightly reduced, about 3 minutes.

4. Arrange shrimp on a bed of the broiled zucchini. Spoon pepper-pineapple sauce on top and serve.

This recipe was excerpted from Rocco DiSpirito's cookbook Rocco Gets Real.

INCLUDES HEALTHFUL RECIPES AS SEEN ON NBC'S **THE BIGGEST LOSER**

ROCCO GETS REAL
COOK AT HOME, EVERY DAY

RECIPES FROM THE SERIES *ROCCO GETS REAL* ON A&E NETWORK

1. To peel shrimp, hold onto the tail firmly and open the shell lengthwise down the body. Starting at the head, gently pull the outer shell from the shrimp. Then hold the shrimp at the head end and gently pull on the tail to remove.

2. To devein shrimp, use a sharp knife to make a slit along the back of the shrimp. Then, using the tip of your knife, gently remove the black vein that runs the length of its back. Rinse the shrimp in cold water to clean; pat dry.

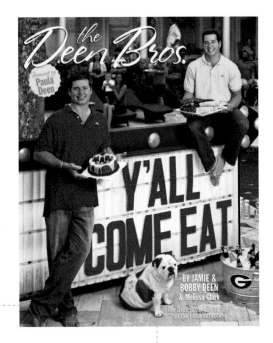

Recipe excerpted from Jamie and Bobby Deen's cookbook Y'all Come Eat

Five-Veggie, Four-Cheese Lasagna

PREP: 30 minutes   **ROAST:** 35 minutes
BAKE: 40 minutes   **MAKES:** 8 to 10 servings

Salt
- 8 ounces uncooked lasagna noodles
- 3 tablespoons extra virgin olive oil, plus additional for drizzling
- 6 ounces portobello mushrooms, sliced into ¼-inch-thick pieces
- I medium zucchini, sliced lengthwise into ¼-inch-thick strips
- I red onion, sliced into ¼-inch-thick rings
  Freshly ground black pepper
- I 14-ounce can artichoke hearts, drained and quartered
- I 10-ounce package frozen chopped spinach, thawed, all excess water squeezed out
- I 26-ounce jar spaghetti sauce
- 8 ounces ricotta cheese
- 4 ounces provolone cheese, shredded (about I cup)
- 4 ounces Parmesan cheese, freshly grated (about I cup)
- 8 ounces fresh mozzarella cheese, thinly sliced (about 2 cups)

I. Preheat oven to 375°F. Bring a large pot of salted water to a boil. Add the lasagna noodles and cook according to package directions until al dente; drain well. Arrange noodles in a single layer on a dish towel-lined baking sheet. Drizzle lightly with olive oil; set aside.

2. Spread the mushrooms on a baking sheet. On a separate baking sheet, spread the zucchini and onion in a layer. Drizzle 1½ tablespoons oil over each; season with salt and pepper. Roast until golden and caramelized (25 minutes for the mushrooms and 35 minutes for the zucchini and onion); cool. In a bowl, combine the vegetables with the artichoke hearts and spinach.

3. In a small saucepan, heat the sauce over medium heat for 5 minutes. Spread one-fourth of the sauce over the bottom of a 13×9×2-inch baking pan. Top with a single layer of lasagna noodles (about one-third), one-third of the ricotta, and an additional one-fourth of the sauce. Spread half the vegetable mixture on top of the sauce, then layer one-third of the provolone, Parmesan, and mozzarella on top of the vegetables. Layer on another one-third of the pasta, another one-fourth of the sauce, the remaining vegetable mixture, and another one-third of all the cheeses. Top with remaining pasta, sauce, and cheeses. Cover the lasagna loosely with foil. Bake 40 to 45 minutes or until bubbling and golden. Remove the foil, increase the oven temperature to 450°F, and continue baking about 10 minutes more or until the cheese is brown around the edges. Let stand for at least 10 minutes before serving.

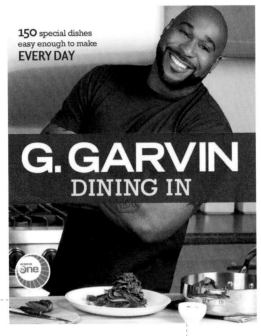

150 special dishes
easy enough to make
EVERY DAY

G. GARVIN
DINING IN

*This recipe was excerpted from
G. Garvin's cookbook* Dining In.

bbq chicken linguine
(*my oscar dish*)

START TO FINISH: 4 servings   MAKES: 4 servings

- 1   pound dried linguine pasta
- 1   tablespoon olive oil
- 1   tablespoon diced shallots
- 1   teaspoon diced jalapeño chile pepper
- 12   ounces skinless boneless chicken thighs, chopped
- ¼   cup chicken stock or broth
- ¾   cup purchased or homemade barbecue sauce
     Grilled Asparagus (see recipe, below)

1. Cook the pasta according to package directions.

2. While the pasta is cooking, heat the oil in a medium sauté pan over medium heat. Add shallots and jalapeño pepper; sauté for 2 minutes. Add the chicken; sauté for 3 to 4 minutes or until chicken is no longer pink.

3. Add the drained cooked pasta, the stock, and half of the barbecue sauce; simmer for 2 minutes then add the remaining barbecue sauce. Serve with Grilled Asparagus.

GRILLED ASPARAGUS: Lightly coat a grill pan with olive oil. Remove tough stems from one bunch (about 1 pound) asparagus. Cut stalks into 2-inch pieces. Drizzle with 1 tablespoon olive oil; season with salt and pepper. Grill for 4 to 6 minutes in grill pan or until asparagus is tender.

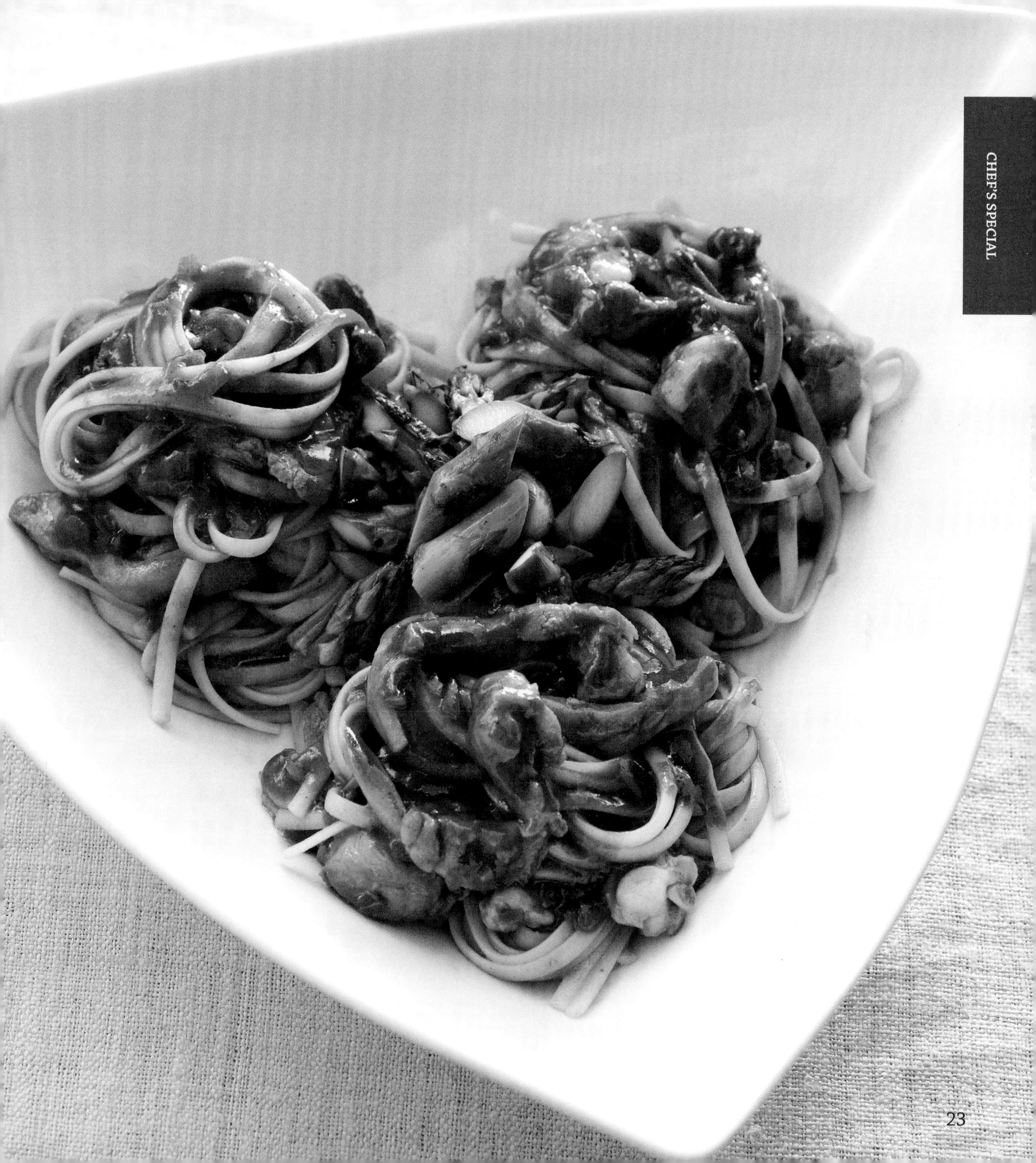

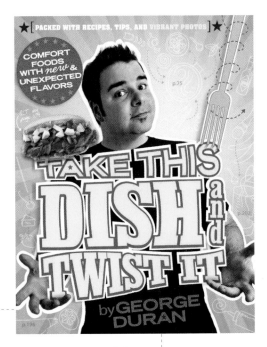

This recipe was excerpted from George Duran's cookbook Take This Dish and Twist It.

Guiltless Oven-Fried Chicken

PREP: 10 minutes   BAKE: 20 minutes   MAKES: 4 servings

- 1 cup low-fat mayonnaise
- 1 tablespoon garlic powder
- 1 tablespoon paprika
- 1 teaspoon chili powder
- 3 tablespoons water
   Kosher salt and freshly ground black pepper, to taste
- 4 chicken thighs, skin removed
   Nonstick cooking spray
- 2 cups panko (Japanese-style bread crumbs)

1. Preheat the oven to 350°F. In a large bowl combine the mayonnaise, garlic powder, paprika, and chili powder. Mix with water, 1 tablespoon at a time, to make it the consistency of whipping cream; season with salt and pepper. Add the chicken pieces; coat well with the mayonnaise mixture.

2. Lightly coat a nonstick baking sheet with cooking spray. Pour the panko onto a plate. Toss the chicken thighs, one at a time, in the crumbs to completely coat. Place the chicken on the baking sheet; coat with cooking spray. Bake for 20 to 25 minutes or until the chicken is browned and cooked through, turning once. Serve with your favorite side dishes.

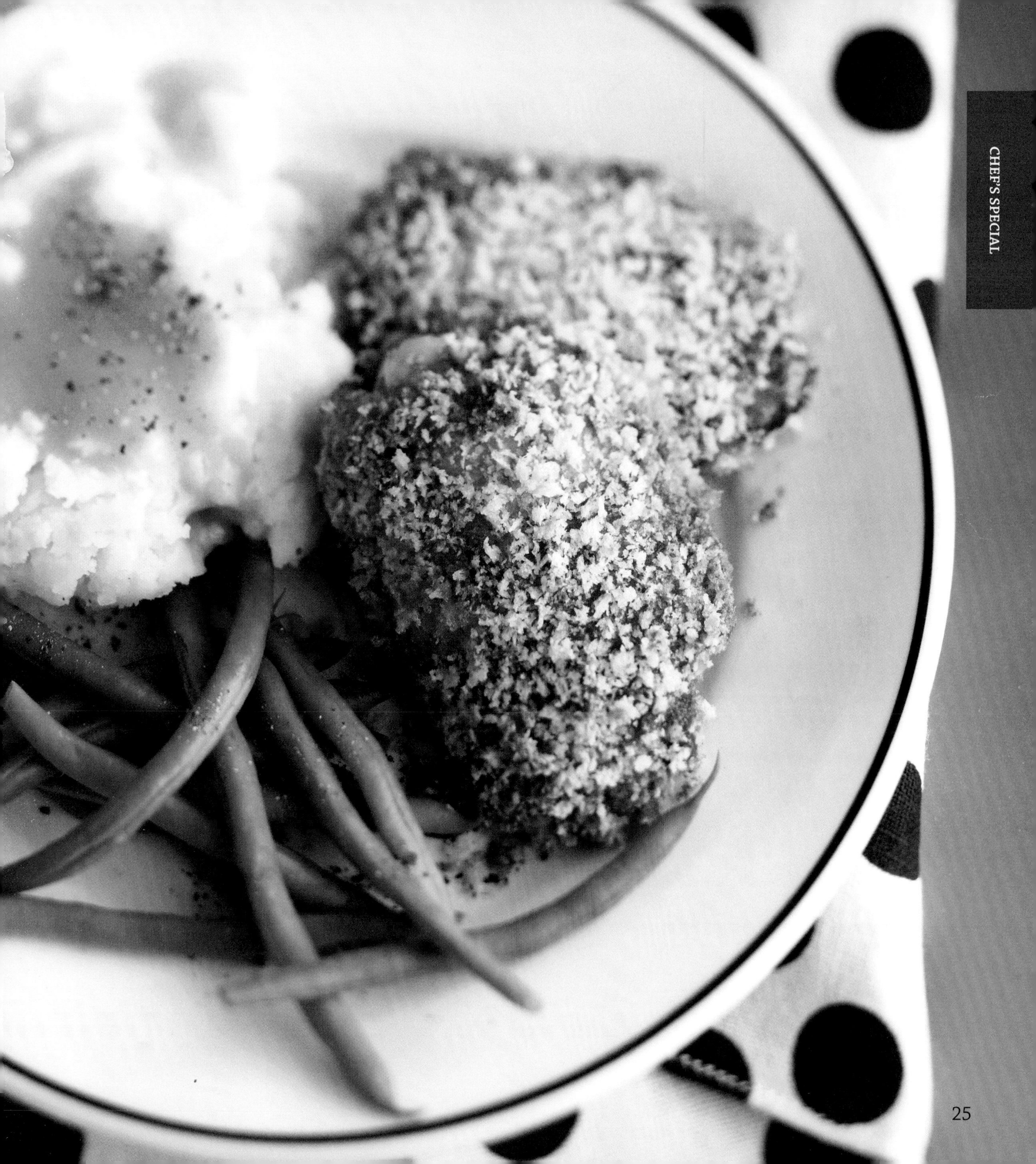

2 Hearty Meats

Get your protein in the most delicious ways—beef, pork, and so much more!

Top Sirloin with Onions and Carrots

START TO FINISH: 1 hour MAKES: 4 servings

    4 slices bacon
    4 small onions, peeled and cut into l-inch slices
    8 small white or orange carrots, halved lengthwise
    4 small red potatoes, cut up (I pound total)
 $^1/_2$ cup beef broth
 $^1/_4$ cup beer, dark beer, or beef broth
    I tablespoon packed brown sugar
    I teaspoon dried thyme, crushed
 1$^1/_4$ pounds boneless beef top sirloin steak, cut 1$^1/_2$ to 2 inches thick
 $^1/_4$ teaspoon salt
 $^1/_4$ teaspoon pepper
       Snipped fresh thyme (optional)

I. In a very large skillet cook bacon over medium heat until crisp. Remove from skillet; drain on paper towels. Drain, reserving about 1 tablespoon of the drippings in the skillet.

2. In skillet cook onions over medium heat about 3 minutes per side or until browned. Remove onions; set aside. Add carrots to skillet; cook about 5 minutes or until light brown, turning occasionally. Remove skillet from heat. Carefully add potatoes, broth, beer, brown sugar, and half of the dried thyme. Return onions to skillet. Return skillet to stovetop. Bring to boiling; reduce heat. Simmer, covered, for 30 to 35 minutes or until vegetables are tender.

3. Meanwhile, season beef with remaining dried thyme, salt, and pepper. Place on the unheated rack of a broiler pan. Broil 4 to 5 inches from heat for 16 to 22 minutes for medium-rare or 22 to 28 minutes for medium, turning once halfway through broiling. Cut into 4 pieces.

4. Remove vegetables from pan with a slotted spoon. Gently boil juices, uncovered, for 1 to 2 minutes or until slightly thickened. Divide steak, vegetables, and bacon among four dinner plates. Spoon juices over. If desired, sprinkle with fresh thyme.

Per serving: 384 cal., I0 g total fat (4 g sat. fat), 87 mg chol., 455 mg sodium, 37 g carbo., 7 g fiber, 35 g pro.

Weeknight Steak with Vegetables

PREP: 15 minutes **COOK:** 16 minutes **MAKES:** 4 servings

2 tablespoons olive oil

2 medium zucchini and/or yellow summer squash, cut into I-inch chunks

I large onion, cut into thick wedges

2 stalks celery, cut into I-inch slices

3 cloves garlic, peeled

I teaspoon dried rosemary, crushed

I pound boneless beef sirloin steak, cut ³/₄-inch thick
  Salt and pepper

¹/₂ cup zinfandel or other fruity dry red wine or beef broth

I 14.5-ounce can diced tomatoes with basil, oregano, and garlic

I. In a large skillet heat 1 tablespoon of the oil. Cook the zucchini, onion, celery, garlic, and rosemary in the hot olive oil over medium heat for 6 to 7 minutes or until vegetables are just crisp-tender, stirring occasionally. Remove from skillet.

2. Cut beef into 4 serving-size pieces. Add remaining oil to skillet. Add beef to hot skillet. Season with salt and pepper. Cook over medium-high heat for 4 to 6 minutes or until medium rare, turning once. (Meat doneness will increase slightly during standing time.) Remove meat from skillet; cover and keep warm.

3. Carefully add the wine to skillet, stirring up browned bits. Add the undrained tomatoes. Bring to boiling. Boil gently, uncovered, for 5 minutes or until slightly thickened. Return vegetables to skillet. Cook and stir until mixture is just heated through. Spoon vegetable sauce over beef to serve.

Per serving: 388 cal., 23 g total fat (7 g sat. fat), 74 mg chol., 362 mg sodium, 16 g carbo., 3 g fiber, 24 g pro.

Wine-Balsamic Glazed Steak

START TO FINISH: 30 minutes   MAKES: 4 servings

- 2   teaspoons cooking oil
- 1   pound boneless beef top loin or top sirloin steak, cut 1/2 to 3/4 inch thick
- 3   cloves garlic, minced
- 1/8   teaspoon crushed red pepper
- 3/4   cup dry red wine
- 2   cups sliced fresh mushrooms
- 3   tablespoons balsamic vinegar
- 2   tablespoons soy sauce
- 4   teaspoons honey
- 2   tablespoons butter

1. In large skillet heat oil over medium-high heat until very hot. Add steak. (Do not add any liquid and do not cover the skillet.) Reduce heat to medium and cook for 10 to 13 minutes or to desired doneness, turning meat occasionally. If meat browns too quickly, reduce heat to medium-low. Transfer meat to platter; keep warm.

2. Add garlic and red pepper to skillet; cook for 10 seconds on medium. Remove skillet from heat. Carefully add wine. Return to heat. Boil, uncovered, about 5 minutes or until most of the liquid is evaporated. Add mushrooms, vinegar, soy sauce, and honey; return to simmer. Cook and stir about 4 minutes or until mushrooms are tender. Stir in butter until melted. Spoon over steak.

Per serving: 377 cal., 21 g total fat (9 g sat. fat), 82 mg chol., 588 mg sodium, 12 g carbo., 0 g fiber, 27 g pro.

Peppery Beef with Crimini Mushrooms

START TO FINISH: 25 minutes MAKES: 4 servings

- 2 to 3 teaspoons steak seasoning blend or cracked black pepper
- 4 beef tenderloin steaks or 2 beef top loin steaks, cut 1 inch thick (about 1 pound)
- 2 tablespoons butter or margarine
- 1 tablespoon olive oil or butter
- 2 4-ounce packages sliced* crimini, shiitake, or portobello mushrooms or one 8-ounce package sliced button mushrooms (3 cups)
- 1 large leek, thinly sliced
- ½ teaspoon dried thyme or oregano, crushed
- 1 5½- to 6-ounce can tomato juice

1. Use your fingers to press the steak seasoning onto both sides of the steaks. If using top loin steaks, cut each steak in half crosswise. In a large skillet, cook steaks in hot butter over medium heat to desired doneness, turning once.

For tenderloin steaks, allow 10 to 13 minutes for medium-rare (145°F) to medium (160°F). For top loin steaks, allow 12 to 15 minutes for medium-rare to medium. Transfer steaks to a warm serving platter, reserving the drippings in the skillet. Keep meat warm.

2. Add oil to drippings in skillet. Add mushrooms, leek and thyme. Cook and stir for 2 minutes. Stir in tomato juice. Bring to boiling; reduce heat. Simmer, uncovered, for 2 to 3 minutes more or until leek is tender. Spoon mushroom mixture over the meat.

*NOTE: If presliced mushrooms are unavailable, slice your own but add about 10 minutes to the prep time.

Per serving: 296 cal., 20 g total fat (8 g sat. fat), 86 mg chol., 419 mg sodium, 5 g carbo., 1 g fiber, 26 g pro.

Cheese-Topped Steaks

PREP: 20 minutes GRILL: 15 minutes MAKES: 4 servings

  2 ounces Gorgonzola cheese or other blue cheese, crumbled (¹/₂ cup)
¹/₄ cup cooked bacon pieces
¹/₄ cup pine nuts or slivered almonds, toasted
  2 tablespoons fresh thyme leaves
  2 cloves garlic, minced
¹/₄ teaspoon freshly ground black pepper
     Coarse salt or salt
  4 boneless beef top loin steaks, cut 1 inch thick (about 3 pounds total)

1. In a small bowl combine cheese, bacon, nuts, thyme, garlic, and pepper; set aside.

2. Sprinkle steaks lightly with salt. For a charcoal grill, place steaks on rack of an uncovered grill directly over medium heat. Grill to desired doneness, turning once halfway through grilling. Allow 10 to 12 minutes for medium-rare (145°F) or 12 to 15 minutes for medium (160°F). (For a gas grill, preheat grill. Reduce heat to medium. Place steaks on grill rack over heat. Cover and grill as above. To broil, place steaks on the unheated rack of a broiler pan. Broil 3 to 4 inches from heat until desired doneness, turning once. Allow 12 to 14 minutes for medium-rare and 15 to 18 minutes for medium.)

3. To serve, top steaks with cheese mixture. Grill or broil 1 to 2 minutes longer to soften cheese slightly.

Per serving: 640 cal., 30 g total fat (11 g sat. fat), 181 mg chol., 616 mg sodium, 3 g carbo., 0 g fiber, 86 g pro.

Beef Hash with a Spicy Kick

PREP: 30 minutes **MARINATE:** 30 minutes **COOK:** 20 minutes
MAKES: 6 servings

- ¹/₂ cup orange juice
- 2 tablespoons lime juice
- l tablespoon adobo sauce (from chipotle peppers)
- l¹/₄ pounds beef sirloin or top loin steak, finely chopped
- 2 cups diced onion
- 2 tablespoons minced garlic (12 cloves) or bottled minced garlic
- l tablespoon chili powder
- l tablespoon cooking oil
- l¹/₂ pounds Yukon Gold potatoes, cooked* and diced
- l tablespoon chopped chipotle peppers in adobo sauce
- 2 Roma tomatoes, seeded and chopped
- ¹/₄ cup snipped fresh cilantro
  Salt and pepper
  Fried eggs (optional)
  Fresh cilantro sprig (optional)

l. In a large plastic bag combine orange juice, lime juice,
and adobo sauce from chipotle peppers; add meat, turning
to coat. Close bag. Marinate in refrigerator for 30 minutes.
Drain; discard marinade. Pat meat dry with paper towels.**

2. In a very large cast-iron or heavy skillet cook the onion, garlic,
and chili powder in hot oil over medium heat for 5 minutes or
until onion is tender. Increase heat to medium-high. Add meat to
skillet; cook and stir about 2 minutes or until meat is browned.
Stir in potatoes and chipotle peppers. Spread in an even layer in
the skillet. Cook for 8 minutes more or until potatoes are golden
brown, turning occasionally. Fold in tomatoes and cilantro; heat
through. Season with salt and pepper. Serve with fried eggs and
fresh cilantro if desired.

*NOTE: To cook potatoes, first wash potatoes. Remove eyes
or sprouts. Cut into quarters. Cook, covered, in enough boiling
lightly salted water to cover for 20 to 25 minutes or until
tender. Drain.

**NOTE: Removing as much moisture as possible from the meat
makes for a crispier hash.

Per serving: 263 cal., 6 g total fat (2 g sat. fat), 45 mg chol., 189 mg sodium,
28 g carbo., 4 g fiber, 24 g pro.

Sesame Orange Beef

START TO FINISH: 25 minutes **MAKES:** 4 servings

- 8 ounces fresh green beans, halved crosswise
- 2 teaspoons sesame seeds
- 1/2 cup orange juice
- 2 tablespoons reduced-sodium soy sauce
- 1 tablespoon toasted sesame oil
- 1 teaspoon cornstarch
- 1/2 teaspoon finely shredded orange peel
  Nonstick cooking spray
- 1/2 cup bias-sliced green onions
- 1 tablespoon grated fresh ginger
- 2 cloves garlic, minced
- 1 teaspoon cooking oil
- 12 ounces boneless beef sirloin steak, thinly sliced
- 2 cups hot cooked brown rice
- 2 oranges, peeled and sectioned or thinly sliced crosswise

1. In a covered medium saucepan, cook green beans in a small amount of boiling water for 6 to 8 minutes or until crisp-tender. Drain; set aside.

2. Meanwhile, in a small skillet cook sesame seeds over medium heat for 1 to 2 minutes or until toasted, stirring frequently. Set aside.

3. For sauce, in a small bowl combine orange juice, soy sauce, sesame oil, cornstarch, and orange peel; set aside.

4. Coat an unheated large nonstick skillet with cooking spray. Preheat over medium-high heat. Add green onions, ginger, and garlic to hot skillet; stir-fry for 1 minute. Add the precooked green beans; stir-fry for 2 minutes. Remove vegetables from skillet.

5. Carefully add oil to the hot skillet. Add beef; stir-fry about 3 minutes or until desired doneness. Remove from skillet.

6. Stir sauce; add to skillet. Cook and stir until thickened and bubbly; cook and stir for 2 minutes more. Return meat and vegetables to skillet. Heat through, stirring to coat all ingredients with sauce. Serve over hot cooked brown rice. Top with orange sections and sprinkle with toasted sesame seeds.

Per serving: 348 cal., 10 g total fat (2 g sat. fat), 52 mg chol., 341 mg sodium, 41 g carbo., 6 g fiber, 24 g pro.

Southwest Beef and Linguine Toss

START TO FINISH: 25 minutes **MAKES:** 4 servings

    4 ounces packaged dried linguine
 ³/₄ pounds beef top round steak
    1 tablespoon cooking oil
    2 teaspoons chili powder
 ¹/₂ teaspoon bottled minced garlic or 1 clove garlic, minced
    1 small onion, sliced and separated into rings
    1 red or green sweet pepper, cut into strips
    2 cups frozen whole kernel corn
 ¹/₄ cup picante sauce
       Fresh cilantro (optional)
       Chili powder (optional)

1. Cook linguine according to package directions. Drain. Rinse with warm water. Set aside.

2. Meanwhile, trim any separable fat from steak. Cut steak into thin, bite-size strips. Set aside.

3. Pour cooking oil into a wok or large skillet. (Add more oil as necessary during cooking.) Preheat over medium-high heat. Stir-fry the 2 teaspoons chili powder and garlic in hot oil for 15 seconds. Add onion; stir-fry for 1 minute. Add the red or green pepper; stir-fry for 1 to 2 minutes more or until vegetables are crisp-tender. Remove vegetables from wok.

4. Add the beef to the hot work; stir-fry for 2 to 3 minutes or to desired doneness. Return vegetables to the wok. Stir in corn and picante sauce. Add the cooked linguine. Toss together to coat with sauce. Cook and stir until heated through. If desired, garnish with fresh cilantro and sprinkle with additional chili powder.

Per serving: 351 cal., 9 g total fat (2 g sat. fat), 54 mg chol., 166 mg sodium, 43 g carbo., 1 g fiber, 27 g pro.

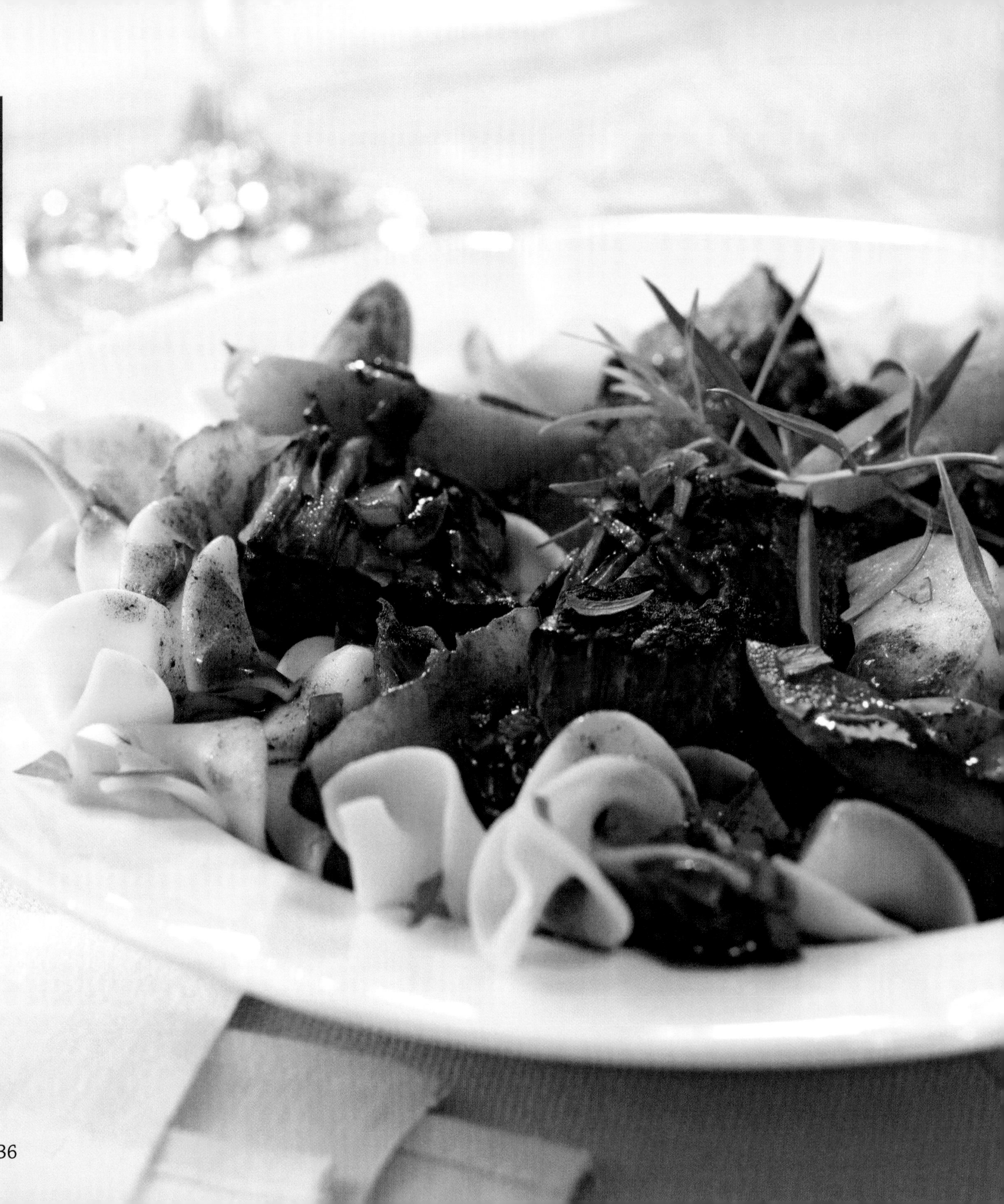

Easy Pot Roast

START TO FINISH: 25 minutes **MAKES:** 4 servings

I 17-ounce refrigerated cooked beef roast au jus
2 tablespoons minced shallots
I tablespoon butter
2 tablespoons tarragon vinegar or white wine vinegar
2 cups fresh, pitted fruit cut into wedges, such as peaches, green plums, and red plums
    Hot cooked noodles (optional)
I teaspoon snipped fresh tarragon (optional)

I. Remove meat from package, reserving juices. In a large skillet cook shallots in hot butter over medium heat for 1 minute. Add beef roast; reduce heat. Cover and heat about 10 minutes or until meat is heated through.

2. In a small bowl stir together reserved meat juices and tarragon vinegar. Pour over meat. Toss fruit over top. Cover; heat for 2 minutes more. If desired, serve with cooked noodles. If desired, top with snipped tarragon.

Per serving: 259 cal., 12 g total fat (5 g sat. fat), 64 mg chol., 459 mg sodium, 19 g carbo., 2 g fiber, 24 g pro.

Stroganoff-Sauced Beef Roast

PREP: 15 minutes **COOK:** 15 minutes **MAKES:** 3 to 4 servings

I 17-ounce package refrigerated cooked beef roast au jus
2 cups shiitake, crimini, or button mushrooms
½ cup dairy sour cream French onion dip
2 cups hot cooked noodles

I. Transfer beef with juices to a large skillet (leave meat in large pieces). Remove stems from shiitake mushrooms; halve or quarter mushrooms. Add mushrooms to skillet. Cover and cook over medium-low heat for 15 minutes or until heated through, stirring mushrooms once and turning meat over halfway through cooking time. Use a wooden spoon to break meat into bite-size pieces. Stir onion dip into meat mixture; heat through (do not boil). Stir in hot cooked noodles.

Per serving: 542 cal., 7 g total fat (11 g sat. fat), 99 mg chol., 787 mg sodium, 46 g carbo., 4 g fiber, 8 g pro.

Individual Sicilian Meat Loaves

START TO FINISH: 35 minutes   MAKES: 4 servings

 1 egg, beaten
 1 14-ounce jar garlic and onion pasta sauce (1¾ cups)
 ¼ cup seasoned fine dry bread crumbs
 ¼ teaspoon salt
 ¼ teaspoon pepper
 12 ounces ground beef
 2 ounces mozzarella cheese
 4 thin slices prosciutto or cooked ham (about 2 ounces)
 1 9-ounce package refrigerated plain or spinach fettuccine
  Finely shredded Parmesan cheese (optional)

1. Preheat oven to 400°F. In a medium mixing bowl combine egg, ¼ cup of the pasta sauce, the fine dry bread crumbs, salt, and pepper. Add ground beef; mix well.

2. Cut mozzarella cheese into four logs measuring approximately 2¼×¾×½-inches. Wrap a slice of prosciutto around each cheese log. Shape one-fourth of the ground beef mixture around each cheese log to form a loaf. Flatten the four meat loaves to 1½ inches thick and place in a shallow baking pan.

3. Bake loaves, uncovered, for 20 minutes or until meat is done (160°F).

4. Meanwhile, prepare pasta according to package directions; drain. In a small saucepan heat remaining pasta sauce over medium heat until bubbly.

5. Arrange meat loaves over hot cooked pasta. Spoon sauce over top and, if desired, sprinkle with cheese.

Per serving: 631 cal., 31 g total fat (12 g sat. fat), 173 mg chol., 1,132 mg sodium, 55 g carbo., 3 g fiber, 31 g pro.

Creamy Beef and Cabbage

PREP: 25 minutes **MAKES:** 6 servings

- 1 pound lean ground beef
- 1 medium onion, chopped (1/2 cup)
- 1 medium head cabbage, cored and coarsely chopped (8 cups)
- 1 8-ounce carton light dairy sour cream
- 1 cup shredded American cheese (4 ounces)
- 1/2 teaspoon salt
- 1/4 teaspoon ground black pepper
- 1 cup soft bread crumbs
- 2 tablespoons butter, melted

1. Preheat oven to 375°F. In a very large ovenproof skillet, cook beef and onion until meat is brown. Drain off fat. Stir in cabbage. Cover and cook over medium heat about 10 minutes or until cabbage is crisp-tender, stirring occasionally. Stir in sour cream, cheese, salt, and pepper.

2. In a small bowl combine bread crumbs and melted butter; sprinkle over casserole. Bake, uncovered, about 20 minutes or until heated through.

MAKE-AHEAD DIRECTIONS: Prepare as directed, except transfer mixture to a 2-quart baking dish. Do not sprinkle cabbage mixture with bread crumb mixture. Cover unbaked casserole; chill in the refrigerator up to 24 hours. Before baking, combine bread crumbs and melted butter; sprinkle over casserole. Bake, covered, in a 375°F oven for 25 minutes. Uncover and bake for 25 to 30 minutes more or until heated through.

Per serving: 328 cal., 28 g total fat (15 g sat. fat), 92 mg chol., 625 mg sodium, 12 g carbo., 3 g fiber, 21 g pro.

Sweet and Sour Meatballs

START TO FINISH: 30 minutes   MAKES: 4 servings

- 1 20-ounce can pineapple chunks
- ³/₄ cup maple syrup or maple-flavored syrup
- ¹/₂ cup cider vinegar
- 1 12- to 16-ounce package frozen cooked meatballs
- 2 medium red and/or green sweet peppers
- ¹/₄ cup cold water
- 2 tablespoons cornstarch
- ¹/₂ teaspoon salt
- 2 cups hot cooked Asian noodles or spaghetti
-    Sliced green onions (optional)

1. Drain pineapple, reserving liquid. Set pineapple chunks aside. In a large saucepan, stir together pineapple liquid, syrup, and vinegar. Add meatballs. Bring to boiling; reduce heat. Simmer, covered, for 15 minutes.

2. Meanwhile, remove seeds from sweet peppers and cut into ³/₄-inch pieces. Add to meatballs. Simmer, covered, for 5 minutes more.

3. In a small bowl stir together water, cornstarch, and salt until smooth. Stir into meatball mixture. Cook and stir until thickened and bubbly. Cook and stir 1 minute more. Stir in pineapple chunks; heat through. Serve over hot cooked noodles and, if desired, sprinkle with green onions.

Per serving: 667 cal., 23 g total fat (9 g sat. fat), 30 mg chol., 972 mg sodium, 107 g carbo., 5 g fiber, 14 g pro.

Pork Loin with Vegetables

PREP: 10 minutes **COOK:** 4 minutes **ROAST:** 35 minutes
MAKES: 4 servings

- 12 ounces packaged, peeled baby carrots (2½ cups)
- 12 ounces tiny new potatoes, quartered
- 1 12- to 16-ounce pork tenderloin
- ⅔ cup apricot preserves
- ¼ cup white wine vinegar or white vinegar

1. Preheat oven to 425°F. Meanwhile, in a medium saucepan cook the carrots and potatoes in small amount of boiling water for 4 minutes; drain. Meanwhile, place the tenderloin in a 13×9×2-inch baking pan. Arrange carrots and potatoes around meat. Roast, uncovered, for 20 minutes.

2. In a small bowl stir together the preserves and vinegar; brush some of the mixture over meat. Drizzle remaining preserves mixture over vegetables; toss to coat. Roast, uncovered, for 15 minutes more or until vegetables and meat are tender and meat juices run clear (160°). Stir vegetable mixture.

3. Cover and let meat and vegetables stand for 10 minutes. Slice meat and place on a serving platter. Transfer vegetables to serving platter with a slotted spoon. Drizzle pan juices over meat and vegetables.

Per serving: 365 cal., 2 g total fat (1 g sat. fat), 50 mg chol., 84 mg sodium, 62 g carbo., 5 g fiber, 23 g pro.

Pork Tenderloin with Mustard Sauce

PREP: 20 minutes **ROAST:** 25 minutes **MAKES:** 8 servings

- ¼ cup sugar
- ¼ cup soy sauce
- ¼ cup ketchup
- 2 tablespoons dry sherry or dry white wine
- 2 teaspoons grated fresh ginger or ¼ teaspoon ground ginger
- 1 clove garlic, minced
- 2 ¾-pound pork tenderloins
- 1 tablespoon sesame seeds
- ⅔ cup dairy sour cream
- ⅔ cup mayonnaise or salad dressing
- 1 tablespoon finely chopped green onion
- 1½ teaspoons vinegar
- 1 to 2 teaspoons dry mustard
- ⅛ teaspoon salt

1. Preheat oven to 425°F. For basting sauce, in a small bowl, stir together sugar, soy sauce, ketchup, sherry, ginger, and garlic.

2. Place pork tenderloins on a rack in a shallow roasting pan. Brush basting sauce over tenderloins. Roast for 15 minutes. Spoon basting sauce in pan over tenderloins. Sprinkle tenderloins with sesame seeds. Roast for 10 to 20 minutes more or until an instant-read thermometer inserted in the thickest part of each tenderloin registers 160°F.

3. Meanwhile, for mustard sauce, in a small bowl stir together sour cream, mayonnaise, green onion, vinegar, dry mustard, and salt.

4. To serve, slice tenderloins and arrange on a serving platter. Serve with mustard sauce.

Per serving: 317 cal., 21 g total fat (5 g sat. fat), 69 mg chol., 729 mg sodium, 10 g carbo., 0 g fiber, 20 g pro.

Smoky Almond Pork Tenderloin

PREP: 10 minutes **ROAST:** 25 minutes **STAND:** 15 minutes
MARINATE: 1 hour **MAKES:** 4 servings

- ¹/₂ cup apple juice
- 2 canned chipotle peppers in adobo sauce, chopped
- 2 tablespoons honey
- 2 tablespoons balsamic vinegar
- 1 12-ounce pork tenderloin
- ¹/₃ cup finely chopped smoked almonds or regular almonds
- 3 cups spring-mix salad greens
- 1 papaya, quartered lengthwise (optional)
- ¹/₄ cup whole and/or chopped smoked almonds or regular almonds

1. Combine apple juice, chopped chipotle peppers, honey, and balsamic vinegar. Set aside ¹/₃ cup of the sauce. Place tenderloin in a shallow dish. Spoon the remaining sauce over pork. Cover; refrigerate for 1 to 2 hours, turning pork once.

2. Preheat oven to 425° F. Remove pork from marinade; discard marinade. Coat pork evenly with the ¹/₃ cup finely chopped almonds. Place pork on a rack in a shallow roasting pan. Roast for 25 to 30 minutes or until an instant-read thermometer inserted in center of meat registers 160°F. Cover with foil and let stand 15 minutes before carving meat. Slice tenderloin into ¹/₄-inch-thick slices.

3. Divide greens and slices of pork tenderloin evenly among 4 plates. Add a papaya quarter to each plate. Stir 2 tablespoons of the remaining whole and/or chopped almonds into the reserved sauce. Drizzle greens and tenderloin slices with reserved sauce. Sprinkle each serving with the remaining almonds.

Per serving: 332 cal., 6 g total fat (2 g sat. fat), 62 mg chol., 570 mg sodium, 19 g carbo., 2 g fiber, 27 g pro.

Pork with Pears and Barley

PREP: 20 minutes **COOK:** 10 minutes **ROAST:** 35 minutes
MAKES: 4 to 6 servings

- 1   1-pound pork tenderloin
- 2   cloves garlic, minced
- 2   tablespoons snipped fresh sage or 2 teaspoons dried sage, crushed
- 6   ounces boiling onions, peeled and halved
- 2   medium red and/or yellow sweet peppers, cut into bite-size pieces
- 1   29-ounce can pear halves in light syrup
- 1/4   cup balsamic vinegar
- 1   cup quick-cooking barley
- 2   teaspoons snipped fresh sage or 1/2 teaspoon dried sage, crushed
- 1/2   teaspoon salt

1. Preheat oven to 425°F. Starting on a long side, split tenderloin horizontally, almost to opposite side. Coat cut sides with the minced garlic and the 2 tablespoons sage. Fold cut sides together; place meat in a 13×9×2-inch baking pan. Place onions around the meat. Layer the sweet peppers on top of the onions.

2. Drain pears, reserving syrup. Slice pears; add to vegetables in pan. Pour vinegar over all. Roast, uncovered, about 35 minutes or until an instant-read thermometer inserted in center of meat registers 160°F.

3. Meanwhile, add water to reserved syrup to equal 2 cups. In a medium saucepan combine syrup mixture, barley, the 2 teaspoon fresh or 1/2 teaspoon dried sage, and salt. Bring to boiling; reduce heat. Simmer, covered, for 10 to 12 minutes or until barley is tender and most of the liquid is absorbed. Spread barley on a serving platter. Slice meat; arrange on barley. Using a slotted spoon, transfer vegetables and pears to platter around meat. Serve with pan juices.

Per serving: 431 cal., 4 g total fat (1 g sat. fat), 73 mg chol., 354 mg sodium, 72 g carbo., 9 g fiber, 29 g pro.

Pork Chops with Raspberries

START TO FINISH: 25 minutes MAKES: 4 servings

- ³/₄ cup reduced-sodium chicken broth
- 1 tablespoon packed brown sugar
- 1 tablespoon white balsamic vinegar
- 1¹/₂ teaspoons cornstarch
- Dash ground allspice
- 4 pork rib chops, cut ³/₄ inch thick (about 1¹/₂ pounds total)
- ¹/₂ teaspoon salt
- ¹/₄ teaspoon ground black pepper
- ¹/₄ teaspoon dried basil, crushed
- 1 tablespoon cooking oil
- 1 cup fresh raspberries

1. In a small bowl, stir together broth, brown sugar, balsamic vinegar, cornstarch, and allspice; set aside.

2. Trim fat from chops. Sprinkle both sides of each chop with salt, pepper, and basil. In a very large skillet, heat oil over medium heat. Add chops; cook for 8 to 12 minutes or until pork juices run clear (160°F). Transfer chops to a serving platter. Cover and keep warm. Drain fat from skillet.

3. Stir vinegar mixture. Add to skillet. Cook and stir over medium heat until slightly thickened and bubbly. Cook and stir for 2 minutes more. Gently stir in raspberries; heat through. To serve, spoon raspberry mixture over chops.

Per serving: 207 cal., 9 g total fat (2 g sat. fat), 53 mg chol., 444 mg sodium, 8 g carbo., 2 g fiber, 22 g pro.

Pork Chops with Plum-Grape Sauce

START TO FINISH: 25 minutes **MAKES:** 4 servings

  4 boneless pork top loin chops, cut I inch thick
 ¹/₄ teaspoon salt
 ¹/₄ teaspoon ground black pepper
  2 teaspoons olive oil
 ¹/₃ cup water
 ¹/₄ cup plum jam
  I tablespoon balsamic vinegar
  2 teaspoons Dijon-style mustard
 ¹/₂ teaspoon chicken bouillon granules
  I clove garlic, minced
  I small plum, seeded and cut into thin wedges
 ¹/₂ cup seedless red grapes, halved
     Snipped fresh chives (optional)

I. Trim fat from chops. Sprinkle both sides of chops with salt and pepper. In a large nonstick skillet cook chops in hot oil over medium heat for 8 to 12 minutes or until juices run clear (160°F), turning once. Transfer chops to a serving platter. Cover and keep warm.

2. Add the water, jam, balsamic vinegar, mustard, chicken bouillon granules, and garlic to the skillet. Whisk over medium heat until bubbly. Remove from heat. Gently stir in plum wedges and grapes. To serve, spoon plum-grape mixture over chops. If desired, sprinkle with snipped chives.

Per serving: 305 cal., 10 g total fat (3 g sat. fat), 83 mg chol., 386 mg sodium, 21 g carbo., I g fiber, 31 g pro.

Pork Au Poivre with Mustard & Sage

PREP: 15 minutes **COOK:** 14 minutes **MAKES:** 4 servings

  I to 2 teaspoons whole black peppercorns
  I to 2 teaspoons whole pink peppercorns
  I to 2 teaspoons whole white peppercorns
  4 6- to 8-ounce boneless pork loin chops, butterflied
 ²/₃ cup whipping cream
  3 tablespoons dry white wine or reduced-sodium chicken broth
  2 tablespoons Dijon-style mustard
  2 tablespoons snipped fresh sage
  I tablespoon green peppercorns in brine, drained and rinsed

I. Coarsely crack the black, pink, and white peppercorns; stir together. Generously coat 1 side of each pork chop with peppercorn mixture; use your fingers to press onto meat.

2. In a heated very large skillet cook chops, peppered sides down, over medium-high heat for 6 minutes. Turn chops and cook about 6 minutes more or until juices run clear (if chops brown too quickly, reduce heat slightly). Transfer chops to serving platter; keep warm. Scrape any burnt peppercorns from skillet and discard.

3. For sauce, add cream, wine, mustard, sage, and drained green peppercorns to skillet. Bring to boiling; reduce heat. Simmer, uncovered, for 2 minutes or until reduced to about ¹/₂ cup. Serve over chops.

Per serving: 416 cal., 25 g total fat (13 g sat. fat), 148 mg chol., 128 mg sodium, 4 g carbo., I g fiber, 39 g pro.

Pork Chops with Pear-Maple Sauce

START TO FINISH: 20 minutes **MAKES:** 4 servings

- 4 boneless pork loin chops, cut ³/₄ inch thick (about I pound)
- ¹/₂ teaspoon kosher salt, sea salt or salt
- ¹/₂ teaspoon ground black pepper
- I tablespoon olive oil
- ¹/₄ cup butter
- 3 tablespoons pure maple syrup or maple-flavored syrup
- 3 tablespoons peach, apricot or plum preserves or jam
- ¹/₂ teaspoon dried basil or I¹/₂ teaspoons snipped fresh basil
- 3 medium pears, cored and thinly sliced

I. Trim fat from pork. Sprinkle chops with salt and pepper. In a large skillet, heat oil over medium-high heat. Cook chops 8 to 12 minutes or until chops are done (160°F) and juices run clear, turning once. Remove chops from skillet; cover to keep warm and set aside.

2. For sauce, in the same skillet melt butter over medium heat. Stir in maple syrup, peach preserves and basil. Add pears. Cook, covered, about 3 minutes or just until the pears are tender and heated through, spooning sauce over pears occasionally. Serve chops with sauce.

Per serving: 427 cal., I9 g total fat (9 g sat. fat), I08 mg chol., 390 mg sodium, 40 g carbo., 4 g fiber, 26 g pro.

Lime Salsa Chops

PREP: 25 minutes **GRILL:** 8 minutes **MARINATE:** 2 hours
MAKES: 6 servings

- ¼ cup finely chopped red onion
- ¼ cup lime juice
- 2 fresh serrano or jalapeño peppers, seeded and finely chopped (see note, page 75)
- 1 tablespoon toasted sesame oil
- 1 teaspoon cumin seed, crushed
- 6 boneless pork loin chops, cut ¾ inch thick
- 4 plum tomatoes, chopped
- 1 small cucumber, seeded and chopped
- 2 green onions, sliced (¼ cup)
- 2 tablespoons snipped fresh cilantro
- 1 tablespoon honey
- 3 tablespoons jalapeño jelly

1. Combine red onion, lime juice, serrano peppers, sesame oil, and cumin seed; reserve 2 tablespoons for salsa. Trim fat from chops; place chops in a plastic bag set in a shallow dish. Add remaining marinade. Seal bag; turn to coat chops.

Chill for 2 to 4 hours, turning the bag occasionally. For salsa, add tomatoes, cucumber, green onions, cilantro, and honey to reserved marinade. Cover and chill until serving time.

2. Drain chops, reserving marinade; transfer marinade to a small saucepan. Add jalapeño jelly to marinade; cook and stir until mixture boils. Remove from heat; set aside. For a charcoal grill, place pork chops on a grill rack directly over medium heat. Grill for 8 to 11 minutes or until juices run clear (160°F), turning once halfway through grilling and brushing with jelly mixture during the last 5 minutes of grilling. (For a gas grill, preheat grill. Reduce heat to medium. Place chops on grill rack directly over heat. Cover; grill as above.) Serve with salsa.

TIP: To broil chops, place drained chops on the unheated rack of a broiler pan. Broil 3 to 4 inches from heat for 9 to 11 minutes or until juices run clear (160°F), turning once halfway through broiling and brushing with jelly mixture during the last 5 minutes of broiling.

Per serving: 211 cal., 10 g total fat (3 g sat. fat), 46 mg sodium, 14 g carbo., 17 g pro.

Apple Butter Glazed Ham

START TO FINISH: 20 minutes MAKES: 4 servings

- 2 medium sweet potatoes, peeled and cut in 1-inch cubes
- 12 ounces Brussels sprouts, trimmed and halved
- 1 to 1¼ pounds sliced cooked ham, about ¼-inch thick, cut into 4 serving-size pieces
- 2 tablespoons butter
- ½ cup apple butter
- 2 tablespoons cider vinegar
  Salt and ground black pepper
  Baguette slices (optional)

1. In a large saucepan cook potatoes and Brussels sprouts in lightly boiling salted water for 8 or 10 minutes or until just tender. Drain.

2. Meanwhile, in a very large skillet cook ham in melted butter over medium-high heat for 4 to 5 minutes or until heated through, turning occasionally. Remove from skillet and place on serving plates with vegetables; keep warm. Stir apple butter and vinegar into the skillet; heat through. Season to taste with salt and pepper. Serve with ham, vegetables, and baguette slices.

Per serving: 513 cal., 16 g total fat (7 g sat. fat), 80 mg chol., 1,664 mg sodium, 71 g carbo., 8 g fiber, 23 g pro.

Potato-Apple-Ham Skillet

PREP: 35 minutes **BAKE:** 30 minutes **MAKES:** 6 servings

3 cups frozen loose-pack diced hash brown potatoes
with onion and peppers, thawed

1 large red apple, cored and chopped

1 small onion, chopped

2 tablespoons water

1 teaspoon dried sage, crushed

1 cup diced cooked ham

1½ cups fat-free milk

1 cup refrigerated or frozen egg product, thawed, or 4 eggs, beaten

½ cup shredded reduced-fat cheddar cheese (2 ounces)

¼ teaspoon salt

1. Preheat oven to 350°F. Press thawed potatoes between paper towels to remove moisture; set aside. In a large ovenproof skillet, combine apple, onion, water, and sage. Bring to boiling; reduce heat. Cook, uncovered, over medium heat until onion is tender. Remove from heat. Stir in potatoes and ham.

2. In a medium bowl combine milk, egg product or eggs, cheese, and salt. Pour into skillet over potato mixture. Do not stir. Bake, uncovered, for 30 to 35 minutes or just until center appears set.

Per serving: 254 cal., 12 g total fat (4 g sat. fat), 21 mg chol., 561 mg sodium, 21 g carbo., 2 g fiber, 16 g pro.

Lamb with Spicy Apricot Sauce

PREP: 15 minutes GRILL: 12 minutes MAKES: 4 servings

    4 lamb loin chops, cut 1-inch thick
 1/4 cup apricot spreadable fruit
    2 tablespoons white wine vinegar
    2 teaspoons Dijon-style mustard
 1/2 teaspoon ground turmeric
 1/2 teaspoon bottled minced garlic (1 clove)
 1/8 teaspoon cayenne pepper
    1 tablespoon grated fresh ginger
    1 teaspoon olive oil
 1/4 teaspoon salt

1. Trim fat from chops; set chops aside. In a small bowl, stir together apricot spreadable fruit, white wine vinegar, mustard, turmeric, garlic, and cayenne pepper. Set aside.

2. In another small bowl stir together ginger, olive oil, and salt. Spoon ginger mixture evenly over chops; rub in with your fingers.

3. For a charcoal grill, place chops on the rack of an uncovered grill directly over medium coals. Grill to desired doneness, turning once halfway through grilling and brushing with apricot mixture during the last 5 minutes of grilling. Allow 12 to 14 minutes for medium-rare doneness (145°F) or 15 to 17 minutes for medium doneness (160°F). Discard any remaining apricot mixture. (For a gas grill, preheat grill. Reduce heat to medium. Place chops on grill rack over heat. Cover and grill as above.)

TIP: To broil chops, place chops on the unheated rack of a broiler pan. Broil 3 to 4 inches from the heat for 10 to 15 minutes or until medium doneness (160°F) turning once halfway through grilling and brushing with apricot mixture during the last 5 minutes of broiling.

Per serving: 188 cal., 6 g total fat (2 g sat. fat), 60 mg chol., 257 mg sodium, 13 g carbo., 0 g fiber, 19 g pro.

Veal Scaloppine with Marsala Skillet

START TO FINISH: 20 minutes **MAKES:** 4 servings

  3 cups fresh mushrooms (such as crimini, porcini, morel,
      shiitake, or button), quartered, halved, or sliced

  4 green onions, sliced ($1/2$ cup)

  2 tablespoons butter

  1 pound veal leg round steak or veal sirloin steak or 2 skinless,
      boneless chicken breast halves ($1/2$ pound total)

$1/4$ teaspoon salt

$1/4$ teaspoon pepper

$2/3$ cup dry marsala or dry sherry

$1/2$ cup chicken broth

  2 tablespoons snipped fresh parsley

1. In a very large skillet cook mushrooms and green onions in 2 teaspoons of the hot margarine for 4 to 5 minutes or until tender. Remove from skillet, reserving drippings. Set aside.

2. Meanwhile, cut veal, if using, into 4 serving-size pieces. Place each piece of veal or chicken breast half between 2 sheets of plastic wrap. Working from center to edges, pound lightly with the flat side of a meat mallet to about $1/8$-inch thickness. Remove the plastic wrap.

3. Sprinkle meat with salt and pepper. In the same skillet cook veal or chicken in the remaining hot butter over medium-high heat for 2 minutes or until no longer pink, turning once. Transfer to dinner plates. Keep warm.

4. Add marsala or sherry and chicken broth to drippings in skillet. Bring to boiling. Boil mixture gently, uncovered, about 1 minute, scraping up any browned bits. Return mushroom mixture to skillet; add parsley. Heat through. To serve, spoon the mushroom mixture over meat. Serve immediately.

Per serving: 253 cal., 9 g total fat (4 g sat. fat), 104 mg chol., 371 mg sodium, 16 g carbo., 1 g fiber, 27 g pro.

3 Pick Your Poultry

No matter what suits the mood—chicken, turkey, or Cornish game hens—there's a dinner here for you!

Chicken with Creamy Mushrooms

START TO FINISH: 30 minutes **MAKES:** 6 servings

    1   pound sliced fresh mushrooms, such as button or shiitake
    3   tablespoons butter
    6   Italian-marinated skinless, boneless chicken breast halves
        (about 2 pounds)
    3   tablespoons rice vinegar or white wine vinegar
    1½ cups whipping cream
    3   tablespoons capers, drained
    ¼   teaspoon freshly ground black pepper
        Steamed fresh vegetables (optional)

I. In a very large skillet cook mushrooms, uncovered, in 1 tablespoon of the hot butter over medium-high heat about 5 minutes or until tender. Remove mushrooms from skillet.

2. Reduce heat to medium. Add the remaining 2 tablespoons of the butter and the chicken breast halves to skillet. Cook, uncovered, for 8 to 12 minutes or until no longer pink (170°F), turning once. Remove chicken from skillet and keep warm.

3. Remove skillet from heat; add vinegar, stirring to loosen browned bits in bottom of skillet. Return skillet to heat. Stir in cream, capers, and black pepper. Bring to boiling; boil gently, uncovered, for 2 to 3 minutes or until sauce is slightly thickened. Return mushrooms to skillet; heat through. Cut each chicken piece in half horizontally to make two thin pieces. Top with mushroom sauce. If desired, serve with steamed vegetables.

Per serving: 456 cal., 34 g total fat (19 g sat. fat), 183 mg chol., 967 mg sodium, 7 g carbo., 1 g fiber, 33 g pro.

Chicken and Asparagus Skillet Supper

START TO FINISH: 20 minutes **MAKES:** 4 servings

- 8 skinless, boneless chicken thighs
  Salt and ground black pepper
- 3 slices bacon, coarsely chopped
- ½ cup chicken broth
- 1 pound asparagus spears, trimmed
- 1 small yellow summer squash, halved crosswise and cut in ½-inch strips
- 4 green onions, cut in 2-inch pieces

1. Sprinkle chicken with salt and pepper. In 12-inch skillet cook chicken and bacon over medium-high heat 12 minutes, turning to brown evenly. Carefully add broth; cover and cook 3 to 5 minutes more or until chicken is tender and no longer pink (180°F).

2. Meanwhile, in microwave-safe 2-quart dish combine asparagus, squash, and 2 tablespoons water. Sprinkle with salt and pepper. Cover with vented plastic wrap. Cook on 100 percent power (high) 3 to 5 minutes, until vegetables are crisp-tender, stirring once. Transfer to plates. Drizzle cooking liquid; top with chicken, bacon, and onions.

Per serving: 320 cal., 18 g total fat (6 g sat. fat), 134 mg chol., 626 mg sodium, 5 g carbo., 2 g fiber, 32 g pro.

Spring Chicken Scallopini

START TO FINISH: 25 minutes **MAKES:** 4 servings

- 4 skinless, boneless chicken breast halves (about 1¼ pounds total)
- ¼ cup all-purpose flour
- ¼ teaspoon salt
- 4 tablespoons butter
- ½ cup dry white wine and/or chicken broth
- ¼ cup sliced green onions
- ½ cup snipped mixed fresh herbs (such as oregano, thyme, lemon thyme, and/or mint)
- ¼ teaspoon coarsely ground black pepper
- ⅛ teaspoon salt*
- Steamed fresh asparagus** (optional)

1. Place each chicken piece between two pieces of plastic wrap. Working from the center to the edges, pound lightly with the flat side of a meat mallet until pieces are an even ¼-inch thickness. Remove plastic wrap. In a shallow dish, combine flour and salt. Coat chicken pieces with flour mixture.

2. In a very large skillet heat 2 tablespoons of the butter over medium heat. Add chicken; cook for 6 to 8 minutes or until chicken is tender and no longer pink, turning once. Transfer chicken to a serving platter; cover and keep warm.

3. Add white wine and/or broth and green onions to the skillet. Cook and stir for 1 minute, scraping up any browned bits from bottom of skillet. Cook about 1 minute more or until wine mixture is reduced to ⅓ cup. Remove from heat. Whisk in the remaining 2 tablespoons butter until melted. Stir in half of the snipped fresh herbs, the pepper, and the ⅛ teaspoon salt.

4. Drizzle wine sauce over individual servings; sprinkle with remaining fresh herbs. If desired, serve with steamed asparagus.

*TIP: If using chicken broth rather than wine, omit the ⅛ teaspoon salt.

**TIP: To steam asparagus, snap off and discard woody bases from fresh asparagus. Bias-slice asparagus into 1-inch-long pieces. Steam asparagus for 3 to 5 minutes or until tender.

Per serving: 317 cal., 14 g total fat (8 g sat. fat), 113 mg chol., 380 mg sodium, 7 g carbo., 0 g fiber, 34 g pro.

Showstopper Chicken Surprise

PREP: 30 minutes **BAKE:** 12 minutes **MAKES:** 4 servings

- 4 large skinless, boneless chicken breast halves (about 1¹/₂ pounds)
- 1 cup shredded smoked Gouda, Edam or cheddar cheese (4 ounces)
- ¹/₂ cup all-purpose flour
- ¹/₈ teaspoon salt
- ¹/₈ teaspoon ground black pepper
- 2 eggs, slightly beaten
- ³/₄ cup fine dry bread crumbs
- 1 tablespoon peanut oil or other cooking oil

1. Preheat oven to 375°F. Using a sharp knife, cut a pocket in the side of each chicken breast half. Stuff each pocket with about ¹/₄ cup cheese. Secure openings with wooden toothpicks, if needed.

2. In a shallow dish stir together flour, salt and pepper. Place eggs in another shallow dish, and place bread crumbs in a third shallow dish. Coat stuffed chicken breasts in flour mixture. Dip floured chicken in beaten eggs, then coat well with bread crumbs.

3. In a large, ovenproof skillet, heat oil over medium heat. Cook chicken 2 to 3 minutes on each side or until browned.

4. Transfer skillet to oven and bake, uncovered, 12 to 15 minutes or until chicken no longer is pink.

Per serving: 417 cal., 15 g total fat 211 mg chol., 1,016 mg sodium, 23 g carbo., 1 g fiber, 44 g pro.

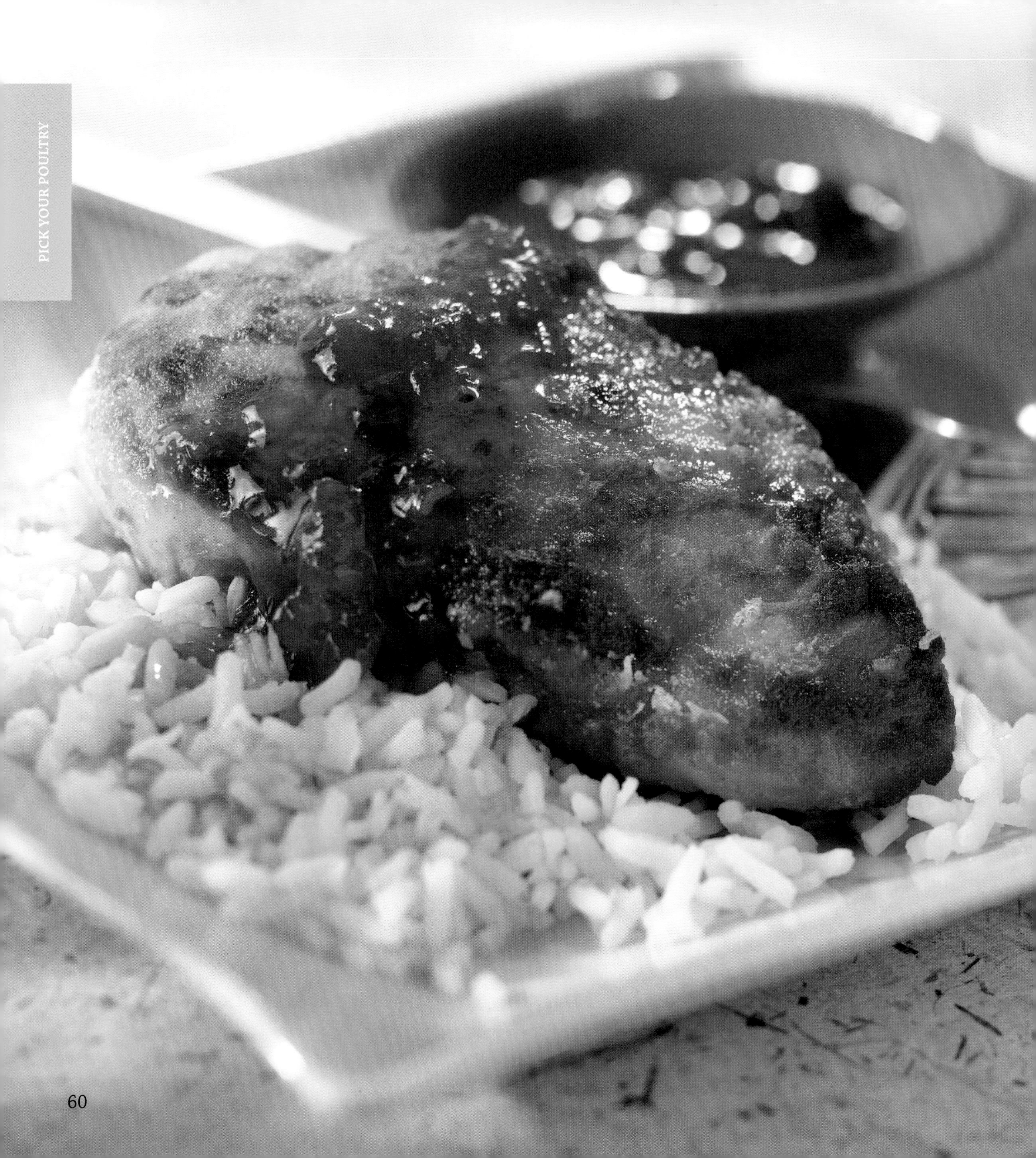

Szechwan-Fried Chicken Breasts

START TO FINISH: 30 minutes **MAKES:** 4 servings

- 1 tablespoon soy sauce
- 1 teaspoon grated fresh ginger
- 1 teaspoon chile oil
- ¹/₂ teaspoon sugar
- ¹/₂ cup all-purpose flour
- 1 tablespoon cooking oil
- 4 skinless, boneless chicken breast halves (about 1¹/₄ pounds total)
- ¹/₄ cup apricot preserves
- ¹/₄ cup chicken broth
  Shredded orange peel (optional)
  Snipped fresh chives (optional)
  Hot cooked rice (optional)

1. In a small bowl, stir together soy sauce, ginger, ¹/₂ teaspoon of the chile oil, and the sugar; set aside.

2. Place flour in a shallow bowl. Brush both sides of each chicken breast half with soy sauce mixture; dip in flour to coat. In a large nonstick skillet, heat cooking oil over medium-high heat. Add chicken; cook for 8 to 10 minutes or until tender and no longer pink (170°F), turning once. Remove chicken from skillet; cover and keep warm.

3. Add apricot preserves, chicken broth, and the remaining ¹/₂ teaspoon chile oil to skillet. Cook and stir over medium heat until preserves melt and mixture is heated through. Spoon sauce over chicken. If desired, sprinkle with orange peel. If desired, stir chives into hot cooked rice; serve with chicken.

Per serving: 315 cal., 7 g total fat (1 g sat. fat), 82 mg chol., 374 mg sodium, 25 g carbo., 1 g fiber, 35 g pro.

Chicken with Quick Cornmeal Dumplings

START TO FINISH: 22 minutes **MAKES:** 4 servings

- 2 tablespoons cooking oil
- ¹/₂ cup all-purpose flour
- ¹/₂ teaspoon ground sage
- ¹/₄ teaspoon salt
- ¹/₄ teaspoon ground black pepper
- 12 ounces skinless, boneless chicken breast halves
- 2 cups frozen mixed vegetables
- 1 14-ounce can reduced-sodium chicken broth
- ¹/₂ cup milk
- 1 11.5-ounce package (8) refrigerated cornbread twists
- ¹/₂ cup shredded Mexican cheese blend

1. Preheat oven to 450°F. Place oil in a large skillet. Heat over medium-high heat. Meanwhile, in a large self-sealing plastic bag combine flour, sage, salt and pepper. Cut chicken into bite-size pieces. Add chicken to bag; seal bag and shake to coat.

2. Add chicken to hot oil; sprinkle any remaining flour mixture over chicken. Brown chicken over medium-high heat for 2 minutes, stirring to brown evenly (chicken will not be completely cooked). Meanwhile, place vegetables in a sieve or colander. Run cold water over vegetables to thaw. Add vegetables, broth, and milk to skillet. Bring to boiling, stirring once. Meanwhile, open package of cornbread twists and separate into 16 pieces.

3. Divide chicken mixture among four 16-ounce individual casserole dishes. Arrange cornbread pieces on top. Sprinkle with cheese. Bake for 9 to 10 minutes or until cornbread is browned.

Per serving: 612 cal., 25 g total fat (7 g sat. fat), 64 mg chol., 1259 mg sodium, 60 g carbo., 3 g fiber, 34 g pro.

Spinach-Topped Chicken

PREP: 30 minutes **BAKE:** 40 minutes **MAKES:** 12 servings

- ³/₄ cup Italian-seasoned fine dry bread crumbs
- ¹/₄ cup grated Parmesan cheese
- 12 large skinless, boneless chicken breast halves (about 3¹/₂ pounds)
- ¹/₂ cup sliced green onion
- 2 tablespoons butter
- 2 tablespoons all-purpose flour
- 1 cup milk
- 1 10-ounce package frozen chopped spinach, thawed and well-drained
- 1 4-ounce package boiled ham slices, diced

1. Preheat oven to 350°F. Combine bread crumbs and cheese; dip chicken breast halves into crumb mixture to coat lightly. Arrange in a 3-quart rectangular baking dish. Set remaining crumb mixture aside.

2. In a saucepan cook green onion in butter until tender. Stir in flour; stir in milk all at once. Cook and stir until thickened and bubbly. Cook and stir 1 minute more. Stir in spinach and ham.

3. Spoon spinach mixture over chicken; sprinkle with remaining crumb mixture. Bake, uncovered, for 40 to 45 minutes or until done (170°F).

Per serving: 211 cal., 5 g total fat (2 g sat. fat), 79 mg chol., 391 mg sodium, 8 g carbo., 1 g fiber, 31 g pro.

Chicken with Peach Salsa

PREP: 10 minutes **GRILL:** 12 minutes **MAKES:** 4 servings

- 2 large yellow and/or white peaches, finely chopped
- 1/2 cup chunky salsa
- 2 tablespoons snipped fresh cilantro
- 4 skinless, boneless chicken breast halves (about 1 1/4 lb. total)
- 1 to 1 1/2 teaspoons ground cumin

1. For salsa, in medium bowl combine peaches, salsa, and cilantro. Cover and chill until needed.

2. Sprinkle chicken with cumin. For a charcoal grill place chicken on greased rack of an uncovered grill directly over medium heat. Grill for 12 to 15 minutes or until chicken is tender and no longer pink (170°F), turning once. (For a gas grill, preheat grill. Reduce heat to medium. Place chicken on grill rack directly over heat. Cover and grill as above.)

3. Serve chicken with salsa.

TIP: To broil chicken, place chicken on the unheated rack of a broiler pan. Broil 4 to 5 inches from the heat for 12 to 15 minutes or until tender and no longer pink (170°F), turning once halfway through broiling.

Per serving: 211 cal., 3 g total fat (1 g sat. fat), 82 mg chol., 250 mg sodium, 12 g carbo., 2 g fiber, 34 g pro.

Sweet-and-Sour Baked Chicken

PREP: 25 minutes **BAKE:** 30 minutes **MAKES:** 4 servings

 8 medium skinless, boneless chicken breast halves (about 2¹/₂ pounds)
   Salt and black pepper
 1 tablespoons cooking oil
 1 20-ounce can pineapple chunks (juice pack)
¹/₂ cup canned jellied cranberry sauce
 2 tablespoons cornstarch
 2 tablespoons packed brown sugar
 2 tablespoons rice vinegar or cider vinegar
 2 tablespoons frozen orange juice concentrate, thawed
 2 tablespoons dry sherry, chicken broth, or water
 2 tablespoons soy sauce
¹/₄ teaspoon ground ginger
 1 medium green sweet pepper, cut into bite-size strips

1. Preheat oven to 350°F. Sprinkle chicken lightly with salt and pepper. In a large skillet heat oil over medium-high heat. Add chicken and cook about 2 minutes on each side or until brown. Transfer chicken to a 2-quart rectangular baking dish. Drain pineapple well, reserving ¹/₃ cup juice. Spoon pineapple chunks evenly over chicken in dish; set aside.

2. For sauce in a medium saucepan whisk together the reserved pineapple juice, the cranberry sauce, cornstarch, brown sugar, vinegar, orange juice concentrate, sherry, soy sauce, and ginger. Cook and stir over medium heat until thickened and bubbly. Pour over chicken and pineapple in dish.

3. Bake, covered, for 25 minutes. Uncover and add sweet pepper strips, stirring gently to coat with sauce. Bake, uncovered, about 5 minutes more or until chicken is no longer pink (170°).

Per serving: 368 cal., 6 g total fat (1 g sat. fat), 82 mg chol., 589 mg sodium, 41 g carbo., 2 g fiber, 35 g pro.

Chicken Breasts with Jalapeño Jelly

PREP: 10 minutes COOK: 12 minutes MAKES: 4 servings

    4 large skinless, boneless chicken breast halves
         (about 1¼ pounds total)
       Salt
       Freshly ground pepper
    2 tablespoons butter
    1 tablespoon water
    2 cups bias-sliced celery
    ¼ cup red jalapeño jelly
    2 tablespoons lemon juice
    1 tablespoon Dijon-style mustard

1. Place each chicken piece between 2 pieces of plastic wrap. Pound with the flat side of a meat mallet to about ½-inch thickness. Remove plastic wrap. Sprinkle chicken with salt and pepper.

2. In a very large skillet cook chicken in hot butter over medium-high heat for 8 to 10 minutes or until chicken is tender and no longer pink, turning once. Remove from skillet.

3. For sauce, carefully stir water into skillet scraping up the crusty browned bits from bottom. Add celery; cook and stir for 1 minute. Add jelly, lemon juice, and mustard; cook and stir about 3 minutes more or until slightly thickened. Return chicken to skillet; heat through.

TIP: For best results, lightly pound the chicken breast pieces using the flat side of a meat mallet. Work from the center to the edges until an even thickness is reached.

Per serving: 281 cal., 9 g total fat (4 g sat. fat), 99 mg chol., 236 mg sodium, 16 g carbo., 1 g fiber, 34 g pro.

Remarkable Country Chicken

START TO FINISH: 25 minutes **MAKES:** 4 servings

- 2 tablespoons olive oil or cooking oil
- 4 medium skinless, boneless chicken breast halves (about 1¼ pounds total)
- ¼ cup chopped onion
- 2 medium tomatoes, chopped
- 2 cloves garlic, minced
- 1 teaspoon dried tarragon, crushed, or 2 teaspoons snipped fresh tarragon
- ¼ teaspoon salt
- ⅛ teaspoon ground black pepper
  Hot cooked linguine (optional)

1. In a large skillet heat oil over medium heat. Add the chicken breast halves; cook chicken for 8 to 10 minutes or until chicken is tender and no longer pink, turning once. Transfer to serving platter; keep warm.

2. Add onion to the same skillet. Cook and stir over medium heat about 3 minutes or until onion is tender. Stir in tomatoes, garlic, dried tarragon (if using), salt, and pepper. Bring to boiling; reduce heat. Simmer, uncovered, for 5 minutes. Stir in fresh tarragon, if using. Return chicken to skillet; heat through. Serve with linguine, if desired.

Per serving: 295 cal., 9 g total fat (1 g sat. fat), 66 mg chol., 210 mg sodium, 23 g carbo., 2 g fiber, 30 g pro.

Chicken Paprika

START TO FINISH: 25 minutes **MAKES:** 4 servings

- 1/4 cup all-purpose flour
- 2 to 3 teaspoons paprika
- 1/4 teaspoon salt
- 4 skinless, boneless chicken breast halves (about 1 1/4 pounds total)
- 2 tablespoons butter or margarine
- 3/4 cup whipping cream
- 1/2 teaspoon bottled minced garlic (1 clove)
- 1/2 teaspoon caraway seeds, crushed
- 1 tablespoon dry sherry
- 2 teaspoons lemon juice
  Hot cooked noodles (optional)

1. In a shallow bowl stir together flour, paprika, and salt. Dip chicken in flour mixture to coat.

2. In a large skillet melt butter over medium heat. Add chicken; cook for 8 to 10 minutes or until tender and no longer pink (170°F), turning once. Remove from skillet; cover and keep warm.

3. Stir whipping cream, garlic, and caraway seeds into skillet. Cook and stir until boiling, scraping up browned bits. Cook for 2 to 3 minutes more or until thickened. Stir in sherry and lemon juice. If desired, serve chicken and sauce with noodles.

Per serving: 409 cal., 25 g total fat (14 g sat. fat), 160 mg chol., 284 mg sodium, 8 g carbo., 1 g fiber, 35 g pro.

Chicken Crunch

PREP: 15 minutes **BAKE:** 25 minutes **MAKES:** 8 servings

    1 8-ounce carton light dairy sour cream
    2 tablespoons lemon juice
    1 tablespoon Worcestershire sauce
    1 teaspoon paprika
    $^1/_4$ teaspoon celery salt
    $^1/_4$ teaspoon pepper
    8 skinless, boneless chicken breast halves (2 to 2$^1/_2$ pounds total)
    1 8-ounce package herb-seasoned stuffing mix (2 cups),
       coarsely crushed
    $^1/_4$ cup butter, melted

I. Preheat oven to 375°F. In a shallow bowl combine sour cream, lemon juice, Worcestershire sauce, paprika, celery salt, and pepper. If desired, lightly pound chicken between 2 sheets of plastic wrap to even thickness. Dip chicken into sour cream mixture to coat, then coat with crushed stuffing mix. Arrange chicken in a large shallow baking pan (pieces shouldn't touch). Drizzle butter over chicken. Bake, uncovered, for 25 minutes or until no longer pink (170°F).

Per serving: 328 cal., 10 g total fat (5 g sat. fat), 90 mg chol., 603 mg sodium, 25 g carbo., 2 g fiber, 31 g pro.

Chicken Fettuccine

START TO FINISH: 25 minutes **MAKES:** 4 servings

    1 9-ounce package refrigerated fettuccine or linguine
    $^1/_2$ cup oil-packed dried tomato strips or pieces
    1 large zucchini or yellow summer squash, halved lengthwise and sliced
       (about 2 cups)
    8 ounces skinless, boneless chicken breast halves, cut into
       bite-size strips
    $^1/_2$ cup finely shredded Parmesan, Romano, or Asiago cheese (2 ounces)
       Freshly ground black pepper
       Finely shredded Parmesan, Romano, or Asiago cheese (optional)

I. Use kitchen scissors to cut pasta in half. Cook in lightly salted boiling water according to package directions. Drain well. Return pasta to hot pan; cover and keep warm.

2. Meanwhile, drain tomato strips, reserving 2 tablespoons of the oil; set aside. In a large skillet heat 1 tablespoon of the reserved oil over medium-high heat. Add zucchini; cook and stir for 3 to 4 minutes or until crisp-tender. Remove from skillet. Reduce heat to medium. Add remaining 1 tablespoon reserved oil to skillet. Add chicken; cook and stir for 2 to 3 minutes or until no longer pink. Add zucchini, chicken, tomato strips, and the $^1/_2$ cup cheese to cooked pasta; toss gently to combine. Season to taste with black pepper. If desired, sprinkle individual servings with additional cheese.

Per serving: 325 cal., 8 g total fat (3 g sat. fat), 108 mg chol., 265 mg sodium, 39 g carbo., 3 g fiber, 26 g pro.

Chicken and Bow Ties

START TO FINISH: 30 minutes **MAKES:** 4 servings

- 8 ounces dried bow tie pasta
- 2 cloves garlic, minced
- 2 tablespoons olive oil
- 1 pound skinless, boneless chicken breast halves, cut into thin bite-size strips
- 1 teaspoon dried basil, crushed
- 1/8 teaspoon crushed red pepper
- 3/4 cup chicken broth
- 1/2 cup oil-packed dried tomatoes, drained and cut into thin strips
- 1/4 cup dry white wine
- 1/2 cup whipping cream
- 1/4 cup grated Parmesan cheese
  Grated Parmesan cheese (optional)

1. Cook pasta according to package directions; drain.

2. Meanwhile, in a large skillet cook the garlic in hot oil over medium-high heat for 30 seconds. Add chicken, basil, and crushed red pepper. Cook and stir for 4 minutes or until browned. Add chicken broth, dried tomatoes, and white wine. Bring to boiling; reduce heat. Simmer, uncovered, about 10 minutes or until chicken is tender and no longer pink. Stir in whipping cream and the 1/4 cup Parmesan cheese; simmer for 2 minutes more. Stir pasta into chicken mixture. Heat through. Pass additional Parmesan cheese, if desired.

Per serving: 574 cal., 24 g total fat (10 g sat. fat), 112 mg chol., 414 mg sodium, 48 g carbo., 2 g fiber, 38 g pro.

Crispy Lemon Chicken Thighs

PREP: 25 minutes **COOK:** 12 minutes **MAKES:** 4 servings

- 1 cup yellow cornmeal
- 1 to 2 tablespoons lemon-pepper seasoning
- 1 teaspoon dried parsley
- 2 tablespoons lemon juice
- 3 tablespoons olive oil
- 8 skinless, boneless chicken thighs (about 1¼ pounds total)
  Lemon slices (optional)
  Fresh parsley sprigs (optional)

1. In a shallow dish stir together the cornmeal, lemon-pepper seasoning, and dried parsley. In another shallow dish, combine the lemon juice with 1 tablespoon of the olive oil. Dip each chicken thigh into the lemon juice mixture; coat thighs evenly with the cornmeal mixture.

2. In a very large nonstick skillet heat 1 tablespoon remaining olive oil over medium heat. Add chicken thighs to the skillet. Cook for 12 to 15 minutes or until chicken is tender, evenly browned, and no longer pink; turning once. (Add more oil during cooking, if necessary.) Garnish with lemon slices and parsley sprigs, if desired.

Per serving: 389 cal., 16 g total fat (3 g sat. fat), 115 mg chol., 935 mg sodium, 29 g carbo., 3 g fiber, 30 g pro.

Chicken with Broccoli and Garlic

START TO FINISH: 35 minutes **MAKES:** 4 servings

- ¼ cup all-purpose flour
- ¼ teaspoon salt
- ¼ teaspoon black pepper
- 4 small skinless, boneless chicken thighs (about 1 pound total)
- 1 tablespoon olive oil
- 1 bulb garlic, separated into cloves, peeled, and sliced (about 10 cloves)
- 1 cup reduced-sodium chicken broth
- 3 tablespoons white wine vinegar
- 2 tablespoons honey
- 1 16-ounce package shredded broccoli (broccoli slaw mix)
- 2 tablespoons coarsely chopped pecans

1. In a resealable plastic bag combine flour, salt, and pepper. Add chicken; seal bag. Shake to coat.

2. In a large skillet heat oil over medium heat. Add chicken; cook for 10 to 12 minutes or until chicken is tender and no longer pink (180°F), turning once. Transfer chicken to serving plate; cover and keep warm.

3. Add garlic to skillet. Cook and stir for 1 minute. Add chicken broth, vinegar, and honey. Bring to boiling; reduce heat. Simmer, uncovered, for 5 minutes. Stir in broccoli. Return to boiling; reduce heat. Cover and simmer for 8 to 10 minutes more or until broccoli is crisp-tender. Stir in pecans. Serve the broccoli mixture with the chicken.

Per serving: 307 cal., 10 g total fat (2 g sat. fat), 90 mg chol., 401 mg sodium, 25 g carbo., 3 g fiber, 28 g pro.

Normandy Chicken

START TO FINISH: 45 minutes **MAKES:** 4 servings

    2 tablespoons butter
    1 large onion, chopped (1 cup)
  ½ cup all-purpose flour
    8 skinless, boneless chicken thighs (about 1¼ pounds total)
    2 medium red tart cooking apples, cored and each cut into 12 wedges
1¼ cups apple cider or apple juice
  ¼ cup dried currants
    1 teaspoon dried leaf sage, crushed
  ½ teaspoon salt
  ¼ teaspoon ground black pepper
       Hot cooked rice, potatoes, or noodles (optional)

1. In a large skillet melt 1 tablespoon of the butter over medium heat; add onion. Cook for 3 to 5 minutes or until tender. Remove onion from skillet; set aside.

2. Place flour in a shallow dish. Lightly coat chicken with flour, shaking off excess. Discard any remaining flour.

3. In the same skillet, melt remaining butter over medium heat. Add chicken. Cook for 4 to 6 minutes or until chicken is browned, turning once. Return onion to pan. Add apple wedges, cider, currants, sage, salt, and pepper. Bring to boiling; reduce heat. Cover and simmer about 15 minutes or until chicken is tender and no longer pink.

4. If desired, serve with hot cooked rice.

Per serving: 364 cal., 12 g total fat (5 g sat. fat), 131 mg chol., 477 mg sodium, 28 g carbo., 4 g fiber, 29 g pro.

Upside-Down Pizza Pie

PREP: 20 minutes **BAKE:** 25 minutes **STAND:** 5 minutes
MAKES: 4 servings

- 1 14.5-ounce can diced tomatoes with basil, garlic, and oregano, undrained
- 2 cups cubed cooked chicken (about 10 ounces)
- 1½ cup sliced fresh mushrooms
- 1 8-ounce can pizza sauce
- 1 cup shredded pizza cheese (4 ounces)
- ¼ cup grated Parmesan cheese (1 ounce)
- 1 11-ounce package (12) refrigerated breadsticks
   Milk
- 1 tablespoon grated Parmesan cheese
   Additional toppings (such as sliced pitted olives, chopped sweet pepper, and/or chopped tomato) (optional)

1. Preheat oven to 375°F. Grease four 12- to 16-ounce individual baking dishes; set aside. In a medium bowl stir together undrained tomatoes, chicken, mushrooms, and pizza sauce. Spoon mixture into prepared baking dishes. Sprinkle pizza cheese evenly over tomato mixture. Sprinkle with the ¼ cup Parmesan cheese.

2. Unroll the breadstick dough. Separate along perforations to form 12 strips. Weave 3 strips over filling in each baking dish to form a lattice crust on chicken mixture. (Depending on the width of your bowls, you may need to cut strips to length or piece strips together.) Brush dough with a little milk. Sprinkle with the 1 tablespoon Parmesan cheese.

3. Bake about 25 minutes or until breadsticks are golden and filling is bubbly. Let stand for 5 minutes before serving. To serve, loosen edges and invert onto plates; remove baking dishes. If desired, sprinkle with additional toppings.

Per serving: 562 cal., 20 g total fat (8 g sat. fat), 88 mg chol., 1,865 mg sodium, 52 g carbo., 3 g fiber, 40 g pro.

Spicy Chinese Chicken with Eggplant

START TO FINISH: 30 minutes **MAKES:** 6 servings

- 4   cups eggplant cut into thin bite-size strips*
      Boiling water
- 2   tablespoons soy sauce
- 1   tablespoon cornstarch
- 1   tablespoon dry sherry
- 8   ounces cooked chicken, cut into bite-size strips
- 2   tablespoons cooking oil
- 4   or 5 fresh jalapeno peppers, seeded and thinly sliced**
- ¹/₂ cup chicken broth
- 1   clove garlic, minced
- 1   tablespoon very finely chopped fresh ginger
- 3   cups hot cooked rice or cellophane noodles

1. In a large bowl cover eggplant strips with boiling water; let stand for 5 minutes. Drain and set aside. (Eggplant may darken.)

2. Meanwhile, in a large bowl combine the soy sauce, cornstarch, and sherry. Add chicken, stirring to coat; set aside.

3. Heat oil in large saucepan; add peppers. Cook and stir for 4 minutes or until tender. Remove peppers from pan. Add chicken mixture to pan; cook and stir for 3 to 4 minutes or until chicken is heated through and sauce has thickened. Stir in eggplant, peppers, broth, garlic, and ginger. Heat through. Serve with rice or noodles.

*NOTE: Peel eggplant, if desired.

**NOTE: Because chili peppers, such as jalapenos, contain volatile oils that can burn your skin and eyes, avoid direct contact with them as much as possible. Protect your hands with gloves, if possible.

Per serving: 17 cal., 7 g total fat (1 g sat. fat), 59 mg chol., 426 mg sodium, 26 g carbo., 3 g fiber,

Turkey Tenderloins with Cilantro Pesto

PREP: 15 minutes GRILL: 12 minutes MAKES: 8 servings

4 turkey breast tenderloins (about 2 pounds)
1¹/₂ cups lightly packed fresh cilantro or basil leaves
¹/₃ cup walnuts
3 tablespoons olive oil
3 tablespoons lime juice
2 cloves garlic, minced
¹/₄ teaspoon salt
Salt and black pepper
Lime or lemon wedges (optional)

1. Cut each tenderloin in half horizontally to make 8 steaks; set aside. For pesto, in a blender or food processor place cilantro, walnuts, olive oil, lime juice, garlic, and salt. Cover and blend or process until nearly smooth.

2. Season turkey with salt and pepper.

3. For a charcoal grill, grill turkey on the rack of an uncovered grill directly over medium heat for 12 to 15 minutes or until no longer pink (170°F), turning once and brushing lightly with cilantro pesto halfway through grilling. (For a gas grill, preheat grill. Reduce heat to medium. Place turkey on grill rack over heat. Cover and grill as above.) Serve turkey with remaining pesto. If desired, serve with lime wedges.

TIP: To broil turkey, place turkey on the unheated rack of a broiler pan. Broil 4 to 5 inches from the heat for 8 to 10 minutes, brushing with cilantro pesto and turning once halfway through broiling.

Per serving: 213 cal., 10 g total fat (2 g sat. fat), 68 mg chol., 134 mg sodium, 2 g carbo., 1 g fiber, 28 g pro.

Stuffed Turkey Tenderloins

PREP: 30 minutes ROAST: 40 minutes CHILL: 4 hours
MAKES: 8 servings

- 4   10- to 12-ounce turkey breast tenderloins
- 4   cups chopped fresh spinach leaves
- 6   ounces semisoft goat cheese (chèvre) or feta cheese, crumbled (about 1½ cups)
- ½   teaspoon ground black pepper
- 2   tablespoons olive oil
- 2   teaspoons paprika
- 1   teaspoon salt
- ¼   teaspoon cayenne pepper

I. Make a pocket in each turkey breast tenderloin by cutting lengthwise from one side almost to, but not through, the opposite side; set aside. In a large bowl combine spinach, goat cheese, and black pepper. Spoon spinach mixture into pockets, dividing evenly. To hold in stuffing, tie 100-percent-cotton string around each tenderloin in 3 or 4 places.

2. In a small bowl combine oil, paprika, salt, and cayenne pepper; brush evenly over tenderloins. Wrap meat in plastic wrap. Refrigerate for at least 4 hours or up to 24 hours.

3. Preheat oven to 375°F. Unwrap turkey and place in a shallow roasting pan. Roast about 40 minutes or until done (170°F). Remove and discard strings; slice turkey tenderloins crosswise.

Per serving: 254 cal., 10 g total fat (4 g sat. fat), 95 mg chol., 478 mg sodium, 1 g carbo., 2 g fiber, 38 g pro.

Turkey Marsala with Mushrooms

START TO FINISH: 30 minutes **MAKES:** 4 servings

- 1 pound turkey breast tenderloin
- 2 tablespoons all-purpose flour
- $3/4$ teaspoon salt
- $1/4$ teaspoon ground black pepper
- 4 teaspoons olive oil or cooking oil
- 12 ounces packaged sliced fresh mushrooms ($4^{1}/_{2}$ cups)
- 1 medium onion, chopped ($1/2$ cup)
- $1/4$ teaspoon dried thyme, crushed
- $1/2$ cup chicken broth
- $1/3$ cup dry Marsala wine or dry sherry
- 1 teaspoon cornstarch

1. Cut turkey tenderloin crosswise into $1/4$-inch slices. In a shallow dish combine flour, $1/2$ teaspoon of the salt, and the pepper. Dip turkey slices into flour mixture to coat.

2. In a large skillet heat oil over medium heat. Add turkey slices, half at a time; cook for 2 to 4 minutes or until no longer pink, turning once halfway through cooking time. (Add more oil as necessary during cooking.) Remove turkey from skillet.

3. Add mushrooms, onion, thyme, and remaining $1/4$ teaspoon salt. Cook and stir for 4 to 5 minutes or until mushrooms and onion are tender. In a small bowl stir together broth, wine, and cornstarch; carefully stir into mixture in skillet. Cook and stir until thickened and bubbly. Cook and stir for 2 minutes more. Return turkey slices to skillet; heat through.

Per serving: 236 cal., 8 g total fat (1 g sat. fat), 68 mg chol., 615 mg sodium, 9 g carbo., 1 g fiber, 30 g pro.

Creamy Turkey Fettuccine

START TO FINISH: 35 minutes MAKES: 2 servings

- 1 pound dried spinach fettuccine and/or plain fettuccine
- 2 8-ounce cartons fat-free dairy sour cream
- ¼ cup all-purpose flour
- 1 cup reduced-sodium chicken broth
- 1 teaspoon dried sage, crushed
- ¼ teaspoon ground black pepper
- 1½ pounds turkey breast tenderloin
- ¼ teaspoon salt
  Nonstick cooking spray
- 3 cups sliced fresh mushrooms
- 8 green onions, sliced
- 4 cloves garlic, minced

1. Cook pasta according to package directions; drain. Meanwhile, in a large bowl stir together sour cream and flour. Gradually stir in chicken broth, sage, and pepper. Cut turkey into bite-size strips; sprinkle with salt. Set aside.

2. Coat a large skillet with cooking spray. Heat over medium-high heat. Add half of the turkey; cook and stir 3 to 5 minutes or until turkey is no longer pink. Remove turkey from skillet. Add remaining turkey, mushrooms, onions, and garlic to skillet. Cook and stir 3 to 5 minutes or until turkey is no longer pink. Return all turkey to skillet.

3. Stir sour cream mixture into turkey mixture in skillet. Cook and stir until thickened and bubbly. Cook and stir for 1 minute more. Serve turkey mixture over hot cooked pasta.

Per serving: 400 cal., 3 g total fat (1 g sat. fat), 51 mg chol., 327 mg sodium, 58 g carbo., 1 g fiber, 34 g pro.

Turkish Chicken Thighs

PREP: 20 minutes GRILL: 15 minutes MAKES: 4 servings

- 1/3 cup purchased chutney
- 1 tablespoon honey
- 1 tablespoon lime juice
- 2 teaspoons spicy brown mustard
- 1 1/2 teaspoons grated fresh ginger
- 1/4 teaspoon five-spice powder
- 8 skinless, boneless chicken thighs (about 2 pounds)
- 1 tablespoon snipped fresh parsley
- 1 tablespoon sesame seed, toasted
- 2 teaspoons finely shredded orange peel

1. Snip any large pieces of chutney. In a small bowl combine chutney, honey, lime juice, mustard, ginger, and five-spice powder; set aside. Trim fat from chicken thighs.

2. For a charcoal grill, place chicken on the rack of an uncovered grill directly over medium coals; grill for 12 to 15 minutes or until chicken is done (180°F), turning once and brushing with chutney mixture during the last 4 to 5 minutes of grilling. (For gas grill, preheat grill. Reduce heat to medium; cover and grill as above.)*

3. In a small bowl combine parsley, sesame seed, and orange peel. To serve, place chicken on a serving platter. Sprinkle with the parsley mixture.

*TIP: To broil chicken, place chicken on the unheated rack of a broiler pan. Broil 4 to 5 inches from heat for 12 to 15 minutes or until chicken is done (180°F), turning once and brushing with chutney mixture during the last 4 to 5 minutes of broiling.

Per serving: 384 cal., 11 g total fat (3 g sat. fat), 181 mg chol., 213 mg sodium, 24 g carbo., 1 g fiber, 46 g pro.

Turkey Pies with Potato Topper

PREP: 35 minutes BAKE: 20 minutes MAKES: 4 servings

- 2 medium potatoes (about 10 ounces), peeled and quartered
- 1 medium parsnip, peeled and cut up
- 1/4 cup plain low-fat yogurt
- 1/8 teaspoon salt
- 12 ounces uncooked ground turkey breast or lean ground beef
- 1/2 cup chopped onion
- 1 10-ounce package frozen mixed vegetables
- 1/4 cup water
- 1 14.5-ounce can no-salt-added stewed tomatoes, cut up, undrained
- 1/2 of a 6-ounce can (1/3 cup) no-salt-added tomato paste
- 1 tablespoon snipped fresh thyme or sage or 3/4 teaspoon dried thyme or sage, crushed
- 1 tablespoon Worcestershire sauce
- 1/4 teaspoon ground black pepper

1. Preheat the oven to 375°F. In a covered medium saucepan cook potatoes and parsnips in enough boiling water to cover about 20 minutes or until tender. Drain well. Mash with a potato masher or with an electric mixer on low speed. Gradually add yogurt and salt, mashing or beating to make potato mixture light and fluffy. Cover and keep warm.

2. Meanwhile, in a large skillet cook turkey and onion over medium heat until meat is browned. Drain well. Stir mixed vegetables and the water into turkey mixture. Bring to boiling; reduce heat. Cover and simmer for 5 to 10 minutes or until vegetables are tender.

3. Stir in undrained stewed tomatoes, tomato paste, thyme, Worcestershire sauce, and pepper. Heat through. Divide turkey mixture among four 12- to 16-ounce individual casseroles or ramekins, or transfer mixture to a 1 1/2-quart casserole. Pipe or drop mashed potato mixture in mounds atop hot turkey mixture.

4. Bake, uncovered, for 20 to 25 minutes or until potatoes are heated through.

Per serving: 279 cal., 2 g total fat (1 g sat. fat), 35 mg chol., 287 mg sodium, 41 g carbo., 7 g fiber, 25 g pro.

Fresh Tomato and Turkey Pizza

START TO FINISH: 23 minutes MAKES: 4 servings

    Nonstick cooking spray
1   tablespoon cornmeal
1   10-ounce package refrigerated pizza dough
3   medium plum tomatoes, thinly sliced
4   ounces cooked turkey breast or smoked turkey breast, cut into thin strips
3   tablespoons snipped fresh basil
1/4 teaspoon coarsely ground pepper
1   cup shredded reduced-fat mozzarella cheese (4 ounces)

1. Preheat oven to 425°F. Coat a 12-inch pizza pan with cooking spray. Sprinkle cornmeal over bottom of pan. Press refrigerated dough into prepared pan, building up edges. Arrange tomato slices and turkey strips on the dough. Sprinkle with basil and pepper. Sprinkle mozzarella cheese on top.

2. Bake for 13 to 18 minutes or until cheese is bubbly.

Per serving: 288 cal., 8 g total fat (4 g sat. fat), 39 mg chol., 449 mg sodium, 32 g carbo., 2 g fiber, 21 g pro.

Turkey-Broccoli Casserole

START TO FINISH: 30 minutes MAKES: 4 servings

- 1 10-ounce package frozen chopped spinach or broccoli
- 1 10.75-ounce can condensed reduced-fat and reduced-sodium cream of celery, chicken, mushroom, or broccoli soup
- 1 cup water
- 2 tablespoons butter
- 1 6-ounce package chicken-flavor stuffing mix
- 2 cups chopped and cooked turkey or chicken
- 1/3 cup milk
- 1 tablespoon grated Parmesan cheese

1. Preheat oven to 400°F. In a large saucepan combine spinach, half of the soup, the water, butter, and contents of seasoning packet from stuffing mix. Bring to boiling. If using spinach, break up with a fork. Cover and simmer 5 minutes.

2. Add the stuffing crumbs to mixture in saucepan; stir to moisten. Spread mixture in four individual au gratin dishes or an ungreased 2-quart square baking dish. Scatter turkey over stuffing. Stir milk into remaining soup; pour over turkey. Sprinkle with cheese. Bake 15 minutes or until heated through.

Per serving: 367 cal., 14 g total fat (3 g sat. fat), 59 mg chol., 886 mg sodium, 30 g carbo., 3 g fiber, 27 g pro.

Cornish Game Hen with Roasted Root Vegetables

PREP: 30 minutes ROAST: 1½ hours MAKES: 4 servings

- 2 medium carrots, cut into large chunks
- 2 medium russet potatoes, cut into large chunks
- 2 medium parsnips or turnips, peeled and cut into large chunks
- 2 small onions, quartered
- 2 tablespoons olive oil
- 2 tablespoons balsamic vinegar
- 2 1½-pound Cornish game hens
- 4 cloves garlic, minced
- 4 teaspoons snipped fresh rosemary or 1 teaspoon dried rosemary, crushed
- ½ teaspoon salt
- ¼ teaspoon coarsely ground black pepper
  Fresh rosemary or sage leaves (optional)
  Pear-shaped cherry tomatoes (optional)

1. Preheat oven to 400°F. In a large bowl combine carrots, potatoes, parsnips or turnips, and onions. Add oil and balsamic vinegar; toss to lightly coat. Spread in a 13×9×2-inch baking pan; cover with foil. Roast for 30 minutes. Reduce oven temperature to 375°F.

2. Gently separate the skin from the hen breast and tops of drumsticks by easing your fingers between the skin and the meat to make 2 pockets that extend all the way down the body cavity and over the drumsticks. In a bowl combine garlic, rosemary, salt, and pepper. Set aside 2 teaspoons of the fresh rosemary mixture (1 teaspoon, if using dried rosemary). Rub remaining rosemary mixture under the skin onto the breast and drumsticks. Using 100-percent-cotton kitchen string, tie drumsticks to tail; tie wing tips to body. Sprinkle reserved rosemary mixture on the skin. Uncover vegetables. Add hens to baking pan.

3. Roast hen and vegetables, uncovered, for 1 to 1¼ hours or until vegetables are tender and an instant-read thermometer inserted into the thigh of the hens registers 180°F (the thermometer should not touch the bone), stirring vegetables once or twice. Remove string. Cover hen with foil; let stand for 10 minutes before serving.

4. If desired, garnish with fresh rosemary or sage leaves and tomatoes. To serve hens, use kitchen shears or a long heavy knife to carefully cut hens in half lengthwise. Remove skin and discard. Serve with vegetables.

TIP: To serve 4, double the recipe and use a 13×9×2-inch baking pan or shallow roasting pan.

Per serving: 345 cal., 12 g total fat (2 g sat. fat), 133 mg chol., 399 mg sodium, 27 g carbo., 5 g fiber, 32 g pro.

Cornish Game Hens with Artichokes and Potatoes

PREP: 20 minutes ROAST: 50 minutes MAKES: 4 servings

    2 tablespoons lemon juice
    1 tablespoon snipped fresh oregano
    2 teaspoons olive oil
    3 cloves garlic, minced
    1 teaspoon snipped fresh thyme
  $^1/_2$ teaspoon salt
  $^1/_4$ teaspoon ground black pepper
    1 9-ounce package frozen artichoke hearts, thawed
    8 ounces small potatoes or tiny new potatoes, quartered
    2 1$^1/_2$-pound Cornish game hens

1. Preheat oven to 450°F. In a large bowl combine lemon juice, snipped oregano, olive oil, garlic, snipped thyme, salt, and pepper. Add artichoke hearts and potatoes; toss gently to coat. Using a slotted spoon, transfer artichokes and potatoes to another bowl; reserve garlic mixture.

2. Rinse hens; pat dry with paper towels. Tie drumsticks to the tails using 100-percent-cotton string. Tie wing tips to the breasts. Brush hens with some of the garlic mixture. Arrange hens on one side of a rack in a large roasting pan. Arrange artichoke hearts and potatoes on the opposite side of rack. Drizzle hens and vegetables with remaining garlic mixture.

3. Place roasting pan on middle rack of oven. Roast about 50 minutes or until an instant-read thermometer inserted into the thigh of each hen registers 180°F and juices run clear and vegetables are tender.

4. Arrange hens on a serving platter. Using a slotted spoon, transfer vegetables to platter. If desired, garnish platter with lemon slices and herb sprigs. Using kitchen shears or a long heavy knife, cut the string between drumsticks and around breasts. Carefully cut hens in half lengthwise.

Per serving: 417 cal., 25 g total fat (6 g sat. fat), 168 mg chol., 418 mg sodium, 16 g carbo., 5 g fiber, 31 g pro.

4 Fresh Fish and Seafood

Salmon, tuna, trout—it's all here and it's all fresh and delicious. So sidle up to the dinner table and get your helping of omega-3's tonight.

Herb-Roasted Orange Salmon

PREP: 20 minutes **BAKE:** 8 minutes **MARINATE:** 3 hours
MAKES: 4 servings

1½ pounds fresh or frozen salmon fillets or steaks (about 1 inch thick)
  1 tablespoon finely shredded orange peel
  ¼ cup orange juice
  2 tablespoons olive oil
  1 tablespoon snipped fresh tarragon or ½ teaspoon dried tarragon, crushed
  1 teaspoon grated fresh ginger
  ½ teaspoon salt
  ¼ teaspoon black pepper
     Orange wedges (optional)

1. Thaw salmon, if frozen. Rinse fish; pat dry with paper towels. Cut fillets into serving-size pieces.

2. For marinade, in a 2-quart square baking dish combine orange peel, orange juice, olive oil, tarragon, ginger, salt, and pepper. Add fish; turn to coat with marinade. Cover; marinate in refrigerator for 3 to 4 hours, turning fish occasionally. (Do not marinate any longer, as this will toughen the fish.)

3. Preheat oven to 450°F. Bake fish, uncovered, for 8 to 10 minutes or until salmon flakes easily when tested with a fork. Spoon cooking juices over fish. If desired, serve salmon with orange wedges.

Per serving: 374 cal., 24 g total fat (5 g sat. fat), 111 mg chol., 371 mg sodium, 2 g carbo., 0 g fiber, 34 g pro.

Herb-Crusted Salmon with Roasted Pepper Cream

PREP: 10 minutes BAKE: 20 minutes COOK: 15 minutes
MAKES: 4 servings

- 4 6-ounce fresh or frozen skinless, boneless salmon fillets
- 3 tablespoons honey-Dijon-style mustard
- 3 tablespoons seasoned fine dry bread crumbs
- ½ cup drained, chopped roasted red sweet peppers
- 1 cup whipping cream

1. Thaw fish, if frozen. Preheat oven to 400°F. Rinse fish and pat dry. Brush one side of each piece with 2 tablespoons of the mustard. Sprinkle with bread crumbs. Place fish, crumb-side up, in a 3-quart rectangular baking dish. Bake, uncovered, for 20 to 25 minutes or until crumbs are golden and fish flakes easily with a fork.

2. Meanwhile, in a medium saucepan combine the remaining 1 tablespoon mustard, the peppers, and cream. Bring to boiling; reduce heat. Boil gently, uncovered, for 15 minutes or until reduced to 1 cup. Serve sauce over fish.

Per serving: 576 cal., 32 g total fat (15 g sat. fat), 227 mg chol., 359 mg sodium, 11 g carbo., 0 g fiber, 57 g pro.

Glazed Salmon

PREP: 15 minutes **COOK:** 5 minutes
GRILL: 4 minutes per 1/2-inch thickness of fish **MAKES:** 4 servings

1/2 cup balsamic vinegar
1 tablespoon packed brown sugar or full-flavored molasses
1 teaspoon tamari sauce or soy sauce
1/4 teaspoon finely chopped fresh ginger or 1/8 teaspoon ground ginger
4 skinless, boneless salmon fillets (6 ounces each)

1. In a small saucepan bring vinegar to boiling over medium heat. Boil gently, uncovered, about 5 minutes or until reduced by about half.

2. Stir in brown sugar, tamari, and ginger.

3. Brush mixture on the salmon fillets. For a charcoal grill, place fish on the rack of an uncovered grill directly over medium coals. Grill for 4 to 6 minutes per 1/2-inch thickness or until fish flakes with a fork, turning and brushing with soy mixture halfway through grilling. (For a gas grill, preheat grill. Reduce heat to medium. Place fish on grill rack directly over heat. Cover and grill as above.)

TIP: To broil salmon, place fish on the unheated rack of a broiler pan. Broil 4 inches from the heat for 4 to 6 minutes per 1/2-inch thickness or until fish flakes easily when tested with a fork, turning and brushing with soy mixture halfway through broiling.

Per serving: 336 cal., 15 g total fat 105 mg chol., 171 mg sodium, 11 g carbo., 0 g fiber, 36 g pro.

Garlic Salmon Fillets

PREP: 15 minutes BAKE: 8 minutes MAKES: 6 servings

- 6 4-ounce fresh or frozen skinless salmon fillets, about 1 inch thick, thawed if frozen
  Coarse salt and fresh ground pepper
- ¼ cup snipped Italian parsley
- ¼ cup reduced-sodium chicken broth
- ¼ cup dry white wine or reduced-sodium chicken broth
- 1 tablespoon extra-virgin olive oil
- 4 large cloves garlic, minced
- ½ teaspoon crushed red pepper

1. Thaw fish if frozen. Preheat oven to 425°F. Rinse salmon and pat dry. Sprinkle both sides of fillets with salt and pepper; set aside.

2. In a small bowl combine parsley, broth, wine, olive oil, garlic, and red pepper.

3. Place salmon, flat side down, in a single layer in a 2-quart rectangular baking dish. Pour parsley mixture evenly over salmon fillets.

4. Bake, uncovered, for 8 to 12 minutes or until the fish flakes easily with a fork. Serve immediately.

Per serving: 135 cal., 6 g total fat (1 g sat. fat), 121 mg sodium, 1 g carbo., 0 g fiber, 16 g pro.

Salmon with Apricot sauce

PREP: 25 minutes **GRILL:** 6 minutes **MAKES:** 4 servings

- 4   fresh or frozen salmon or halibut steaks, ³/₄ inch thick (about I¹/₄ pounds)
- 4   fresh apricots or 8 dried apricot halves
- ¹/₂ cup apricot nectar
- ¹/₃ cup apricot preserves
- 3   tablespoons sliced green onions
- I¹/₂ teaspoons snipped fresh oregano or ¹/₂ teaspoon dried oregano, crushed
- ¹/₈ teaspoon salt
   Few dashes bottled hot pepper sauce
- I   tablespoon olive oil
- I   to 2 teaspoon bottled hot pepper sauce
   Salt and ground black pepper
   Nonstick cooking spray
   Fresh oregano sprigs (optional)

I. Thaw fish, if frozen. Quarter and pit fresh apricots; set aside. (Or halve the dried apricots; cover with boiling water. Let stand while sauce and fish are being prepared.)

2. For sauce, in a small saucepan combine apricot nectar, preserves, green onions, oregano, and the ¹/₈ teaspoon salt. Bring just to boiling, stirring frequently; reduce heat. Boil gently, uncovered, about 8 minutes or until sauce thickens slightly. Remove from heat; reserve ¹/₄ cup sauce to brush on fish. In a small bowl combine remaining sauce, apricot quarters or halves, and a few dashes of hot pepper sauce. (If using dried apricots, drain well before adding.) Cover sauce and keep warm.

3. In a small bowl stir together the olive oil and 1 to 2 teaspoons bottled hot pepper sauce. Brush both sides of fish with the oil mixture. Sprinkle fish lightly with salt and pepper.

4. Spray an unheated grill rack with cooking spray. For a charcoal grill, place salmon on the rack of an uncovered grill directly over medium coals; grill for 6 to 9 minutes or until fish just flakes easily when tested with a fork, turning once halfway through grilling. Brush salmon with the reserved ¹/₄ cup sauce during the last 2 to 3 minutes of grilling time. (For a gas grill, preheat grill. Reduce heat to medium. Place salmon on grill rack directly over heat. Cover and grill as above.)

5. Remove salmon to serving platter. Spoon chunky apricot sauce over salmon. Top with oregano sprigs.

TIP: To broil salmon, place salmon on the greased unheated rack of a broiler pan. Broil 4 inches from the heat for 6 to 9 minutes or until fish flakes easily when tested with a fork, turning once halfway through broiling.

Per serving: 304 cal., 8 g total fat (I g sat. fat), 73 mg chol., 260 mg sodium, 27 g carbo., 2 g fiber, 29 g pro.

Pesce Italiano

PREP: 20 minutes **COOK:** 6 minutes **MAKES:** 4 servings

- 2   cups dried penne pasta (about 6 ounces)
- 4   fresh salmon, tuna, or swordfish steaks, ³/₄-inch thick (about I¹/₂ pounds)
- 2   teaspoons Creole seasoning
- 2   cups sliced fresh mushrooms
- ¹/₂ cup dry white wine or chicken broth
- ¹/₃ cup prepared or purchased basil pesto
- 2   tablespoons lemon juice
- I   tablespoon drained capers
- 2   tablespoons olive oil

I. In a large saucepan cook the pasta in lightly salted boiling water for 4 minutes; drain and set aside. (Pasta will not be tender.)

2. Meanwhile, sprinkle both sides of the fish steaks with the Creole seasoning; set aside. (If using a salt-free Creole seasoning, sprinkle fish with ¹/₂ teaspoon salt.) In a large bowl combine the partially cooked pasta, mushrooms, wine, pesto, lemon juice, and capers; set aside.

3. In a very large skillet cook the fish steaks in the hot oil over medium-high heat for 1 minute; turn and cook 1 minute more. Reduce heat to medium. Spoon the pasta mixture around the tuna steaks in the skillet. Bring to boiling; reduce heat. Simmer, covered, over medium heat for 6 to 9 minutes or until fish flakes easily when tested with a fork.

Per serving: 627 cal., 30 g total fat (5 g sat. fat), I09 mg chol., 352 mg sodium, 36 g carbo., 2 g fiber, 46 g pro.

Drunken Fish

PREP: 30 minutes **BAKE:** 20 minutes **MAKES:** 4 servings

- 4 fresh or frozen salmon, halibut, or swordfish steaks, cut I inch thick (about I-¹/₄ pounds)
- ¹/₂ cup chopped onion (I medium)
- 2 cloves garlic, minced
- I tablespoon olive oil or cooking oil
- 2 cups chopped tomatoes (2 large) or one 14.5-ounce can diced tomatoes, undrained
- 2 to 3 tablespoons chili powder
- ¹/₂ teaspoon dried oregano, crushed
- ¹/₄ teaspoon salt
- ¹/₄ teaspoon ground cumin
- ¹/₄ cup tequila or dry red wine
  Salt and ground black pepper.
- 3 cups hot cooked rice (optional)

I. Thaw fish, if frozen. Rinse fish; pat dry. Set aside.

2. Preheat oven to 350°F. For sauce, in a medium saucepan cook onion and garlic in hot oil until tender. Stir in chopped tomatoes or undrained canned tomatoes, chili powder, oregano, salt, and cumin. Add tequila. Bring to boiling. Reduce heat and simmer, covered, for 10 minutes.

3. Place fish in a greased 2-quart rectangular baking dish. Spoon about ¹/₂ cup of the sauce over fish (cover remaining sauce and keep warm). Bake fish, covered, 20 to 25 minutes or until fish flakes easily when tested with a fork.

4. Carefully transfer the fish to a serving platter. Season to taste with salt and ground black pepper. If desired, serve with hot cooked rice. Pass remaining sauce.

Per serving: 242 cal., 9 g total fat (2 g sat. fat), 25 mg chol., 300 mg sodium, II g carbo., 4 g fiber, 22 g pro.

Asparagus-Salmon Scramble

PREP: 25 minutes **BAKE:** 18 minutes per batch **STAND:** 1 hour
MAKES: 8 servings

- I 17.3-ounce package frozen puff pastry (2 sheets)
- I egg yolk
- I teaspoon water
- I pound fresh asparagus, trimmed
- 8 eggs
- ¹/₂ cup milk, half-and-half, or light cream
- I teaspoon snipped fresh dill or ¹/₄ teaspoon dried dillweed
- ¹/₂ teaspoon salt
- ¹/₈ teaspoon pepper
- I tablespoon butter
- 4 ounces havarti cheese with dill, shredded (I cup)
- I 4-ounce piece smoked salmon, broken into chunks, with skin and bones removed
  Fresh dill sprigs (optional)

I. Thaw the pastry sheets at room temperature for 1 hour.

2. Preheat oven to 400°F. In a small bowl mix egg yolk with the 1 teaspoon water; set aside. Unfold the pastry sheets on a lightly floured surface. Roll gently to flatten creases (you should have a 10-inch square). Cut one ¹/₂-inch strip from all 4 sides of each pastry sheet. Brush the edges of the pastry sheets with the egg mixture. Place the cut strips on top and along edges of the pastry sheets, gently pressing in place to form a raised rim; trim ends. Place pastries on 2 baking sheets. Prick the centers with a fork. Brush pastries with egg mixture. Bake, 1 sheet at a time, about 15 minutes or until puffed and golden brown. Cool on baking sheets on wire racks.

3. Meanwhile, in a large skillet bring 1 cup water and a dash salt to boiling. Add asparagus and cook, covered, for 1 minute. Drain. Rinse asparagus with cold water; drain well. Transfer the asparagus to a cutting board. Slice 3-inch pieces from the tips of asparagus; set aside. Cut remaining asparagus into 2-inch pieces.

4. In a large mixing bowl whisk the eggs, milk, snipped dill, salt, and pepper together until well combined. In the large skillet melt butter over medium heat. Add egg mixture to skillet. Cook over medium heat without stirring, until mixture begins to set on bottom and around edges. With a spatula or a large spoon, lift and fold the partially cooked egg mixture so that the uncooked portion flows underneath. Continue cooking over medium heat for 2 to 3 minutes or until the egg mixture is cooked but still glossy. Remove the scrambled egg mixture from heat; fold in ¹/₂ cup of the cheese.

5. Spoon egg mixture into baked pastry shells on baking sheets. Top with the 2-inch asparagus pieces, salmon, and remaining ¹/₂ cup cheese. Arrange asparagus tips over all. Return 1 baking sheet at a time to oven and bake 3 to 5 minutes or until cheese is melted and filling is heated through. Garnish with fresh dill sprigs.

Per serving: 524 cal., 37 g total fat (9 g sat. fat), 265 mg chol., 567 mg sodium, 30 g carbo., 2 g fiber, 18 g pro.

Salmon Potato Cakes

PREP: 20 minutes COOK: 8 minutes MAKES: 6 servings

    I pound fresh or frozen salmon fillets, thawed
    3 cups frozen shredded hash brown potatoes, thawed
    2 eggs, slightly beaten
    I tablespoon Old Bay seasoning
    2 tablespoons butter

I. Thaw fish, if frozen. Rinse fish and pat dry. In a large skillet cook the fish, covered, in a small amount of boiling water for 6 to 9 minutes or until fish flakes easily when tested with a fork. Remove skin, if present. Place the fish in a large bowl and flake with a fork; cool slightly.

2. Add the potatoes, eggs, and seasoning to the fish; stir gently to combine. Using about 1/2 cup for each, form fish mixture into 6 patties. In a 12-inch skillet cook the patties in hot butter over medium heat for 4 minutes per side or until browned and heated through.

Per serving: 235 cal., 9 g total fat (4 g sat. fat), 121 mg chol., 466 mg sodium, 19 g carbo., I g fiber, 19 g pro.

Grilled Red Trout with Apple Salad

PREP: 25 minutes CHILL: up to 1 hour
GRILL: 6 minutes MAKES: 6 servings

    2 Granny Smith apples, cored and chopped (2 cups)
    ¾ cup chopped celery
    ¼ cup pine nuts or chopped almonds, toasted
    ¼ cup lemon-flavored olive oil or ¼ cup olive oil plus I teaspoon finely shredded lemon peel
    3 tablespoons white wine vinegar or cider vinegar
    I tablespoon snipped fresh sage or I teaspoon dried leaf sage, crushed
    ¼ teaspoon salt
    ⅛ teaspoon freshly ground black pepper
    2 tablespoons butter
    6 6- to 8-ounce trout fillets

I. In a medium bowl combine apple, celery, and pine nuts. In a small bowl whisk together oil, vinegar, sage, the ¼ teaspoon salt, and ⅛ teaspoon pepper; toss with apple mixture. Cover and refrigerate up to 1 hour.

2. In a 12-inch skillet melt the butter over medium-high heat. Sprinkle boned side of fish with salt and pepper. Add 2 or 3 fillets to skillet; cook for 3 minutes. Turn and cook for 3 minutes more or until fish flakes easily when tested with a fork. Transfer to serving platter and cover to keep warm. Repeat with remaining fillets, adding more butter, if necessary, and reducing heat slightly if fish begins to brown too quickly.

3. Serve fish with apple salad.

NOTE: To grill the fish, melt butter and brush on boned side of fillets; sprinkle with salt and pepper. For a charcoal grill, place fish on the greased rack of an uncovered grill directly over medium coals; grill for 6 to 8 minutes or until fish flakes easily when tested with a fork, turning halfway through grilling with a wide metal spatula. Or grill fish, half at a time, in a greased grill basket. (For a gas grill, preheat grill. Reduce heat to medium. Place fish on grill rack directly over heat. Cover and grill as above.)

Per serving: 358 cal., 23 g total fat (6 g sat. fat), 151 mg chol., 299 mg sodium, 9 g carbo., 2 g dietary fiber, 30 g protein.

Halibut with Creamy Dijon Sauce

PREP: 20 minutes **BROIL:** 8 minutes **MAKES:** 4 servings

    4   fresh or frozen halibut or sea bass steaks, cut 1 inch thick
        (about 1¹/₂ pounds)
    1   tablespoon butter, melted
  ¹/₄   teaspoon onion salt
  ¹/₄   teaspoon dried marjoram, crushed
  ¹/₄   teaspoon dried thyme, crushed
  ¹/₂   cup dairy sour cream
    1   tablespoon all-purpose flour
    1   tablespoon Dijon-style mustard
  ¹/₈   teaspoon salt
  ¹/₈   teaspoon ground black pepper
  ¹/₈   teaspoon dried thyme, crushed
  ¹/₂   cup chicken or vegetable broth
    4   cups shredded spinach (5 ounces)
    1   medium carrot, shredded (¹/₂ cup)
        Lemon wedges (optional)

1. Thaw fish, if frozen. Rinse fish; pat dry with paper towels. Set aside.

2. For basting sauce, combine butter, onion salt, marjoram, and ¹/₄ teaspoon thyme.

3. Place fish steaks on the rack of an unheated broiler pan. Brush with basting sauce. Broil 4 inches from the heat for 8 to 12 minutes or until fish flakes easily with a fork, turning and brushing once with the remaining basting sauce halfway through broiling.

4. Meanwhile, for Dijon sauce, in a small saucepan stir together the sour cream, flour, mustard, salt, pepper, and ¹/₈ teaspoon thyme. Add broth, stirring until well mixed. Cook and stir over medium heat until thickened and bubbly. Cook and stir for 1 minute more. Keep warm.

5. Toss together spinach and carrot. Line dinner plates with the spinach mixture. Arrange fish on spinach mixture. Top with Dijon sauce. If desired, garnish with lemon wedges.

Per serving: 282 cal., 9 g total fat (2 g sat. fat), 59 mg chol., 549 mg sodium, 9 g carbo., 39 g pro.

Herb-Buttered Fish Steaks

PREP: 10 minutes BROIL: 8 minutes MAKES: 4 servings

- 4 small fresh or frozen halibut, salmon, shark, or swordfish steaks, cut 1 inch thick (about 1 pound total)
- 2 tablespoons butter, softened
- 1 teaspoon finely shredded lime or lemon peel
- 1 teaspoon lime juice or lemon juice
- 1 teaspoon snipped fresh tarragon or rosemary or $1/4$ teaspoon dried tarragon or rosemary, crushed
- 1 teaspoon butter, melted

1. Thaw fish, if frozen. Rinse fish; pat dry. For the herb butter, in a small mixing bowl stir together the 2 tablespoons butter, the lime peel, lime juice, and tarragon. Set aside.

2. Place the fish steaks on the lightly greased rack of a broiler pan. Brush with the 1 teaspoon melted butter. Broil 4 to 5 inches from the heat for 8 to 12 minutes or until fish flakes easily when tested with a fork, turning once halfway through broiling. To serve, top with herb butter.

Per serving: 184 cal., 9 g total fat (2 g sat. fat), 36 mg chol., 140 mg sodium, 0 g carbo., 0 g fiber, 24 g pro.

Red Snapper with Cilantro-Lime Vinaigrette

PREP: 15 minutes **BROIL:** 8 minutes **MARINATE:** 30 minutes
MAKES: 4 servings

2 limes
¼ cup olive oil
2 tablespoons sugar
2 tablespoons red wine vinegar
1 shallot, finely chopped (optional)
1 tablespoon snipped fresh cilantro
1 clove garlic, minced
4 skinned red snapper or other firm white-fleshed fish fillets (about 1½ pounds total), 1 inch thick

1. Finely shred enough lime peel to make ½ teaspoon. Squeeze enough juice from one lime to make 2 tablespoons. Cut the remaining lime into wedges; set aside. In a small bowl, combine the lime peel, lime juice, olive oil, sugar, vinegar, shallot (if desired), cilantro, and garlic. Reserve 2 tablespoons of the oil mixture until ready to serve.

2. Rinse fish; pat dry with paper towels. Place fish in a shallow dish; pour the remaining oil mixture over fish. Cover and marinate in the refrigerator for 30 to 60 minutes. Drain fish, reserving marinade.

3. Place fish on the greased, unheated rack of a broiler pan. Broil about 4 inches from the heat for 8 to 12 minutes or until fish flakes easily when tested with a fork, turning and brushing once with marinade halfway through broiling. Discard any remaining marinade.

4. Transfer fish to 4 dinner plates; drizzle with the reserved 2 tablespoons oil mixture. Serve with lime wedges.

TIP: If you prefer to grill the fish, place on the greased rack of an uncovered charcoal grill directly over medium coals. (If you like, use a greased grill basket to hold the fish.) Grill for 8 to 12 minutes, turning and brushing once with marinade halfway through grilling. (Or, preheat a gas grill. Reduce heat to medium. Place fish on greased grill rack over heat. Cover and grill as above.)

Per serving: 49 cal., 9 g total fat (1 g sat. fat), 62 mg chol., 110 mg sodium, 6 g carbo., 1 g fiber, 35 g pro.

Red Snapper & Vegetables en Papillote

PREP: 20 minutes **COOK:** 12 minutes **MAKES:** 4 servings

4   6-ounce fresh or frozen red snapper fillets (with skin),
     ¹/₂ to ³/₄ inch thick
12 ounces whole tiny new potatoes or Yukon gold potatoes, quartered
2   cups broccoli florets
¹/₃ cup purchased basil pesto
     Aluminum foil or parchment paper

1. Thaw fish, if frozen. Rinse fish; pat dry. If desired, remove and discard skin from fish; set fish aside.

2. Preheat oven to 400°F. In a microwave-safe medium bowl microwave potatoes, covered, on 100-percent power (high) for 5 to 7 minutes or until nearly tender, stirring once. Add broccoli and about half of the pesto; toss to coat.

3. Tear off four 12-inch square of aluminum foil or parchment paper. Divide vegetable mixture into 4 portions, placing a portion in the center of each square. Top each with a fish fillet, tucking under any thin edges of fillets. Spoon remaining pesto over fillets.

4. Bring up opposite edges of foil or parchment paper and seal with a double fold. Fold remaining edges together to enclose mixture, leaving space for steam to build. Place packets on a shallow baking pan.

5. Bake until fish flakes easily when tested with a fork (allow 12 minutes for ¹/₂-inch fillets and 15 minutes for ³/₄-inch fillets.) To serve, carefully slit packets open with a knife.

Per serving: 364 cal., 12 g total fat (2 g sat. fat), 66 mg chol., 270 mg sodium, 17 g carbo., 3 g fiber, 40 g pro.

Lemon-Herb Swordfish Steaks

PREP: 15 minutes GRILL: 8 minutes MARINATE: 30 minutes
MAKES: 4 to 6 servings

- 1½ pounds fresh or frozen swordfish, tuna, or shark steaks, cut 1 inch thick, thawed if frozen
- ¼ cup snipped fresh parsley
- ¼ cup chicken broth
- 1 teaspoon finely shredded lemon peel
- 2 tablespoons fresh lemon juice
- 1 tablespoon fresh snipped rosemary
- 1 tablespoon olive oil
- 1 shallot, finely chopped
- 3 cloves garlic, minced
- 1½ teaspoons fresh snipped tarragon
- ¼ teaspoon salt

1. Place fish steaks in a self-sealing plastic bag set in a shallow dish. For marinade, combine parsley, chicken broth, lemon peel, lemon juice, rosemary, oil, shallot, garlic, tarragon, and salt. Pour marinade over fish steaks. Seal bag. Marinate at room temperature for 30 minutes, turning occasionally.

2. Drain fish steaks, reserving marinade. For a charcoal grill, place fish directly on an oiled grill rack over medium coals; grill for 5 minutes, brushing once with reserved marinade. Discard any remaining marinade. Turn fish and grill 3 to 7 minutes more of until fish flakes easily when tested with a fork. (For a gas grill, preheat grill. Reduce heat to medium. Place fish steaks on grill rack directly over heat. Cover and grill as above.)

NOTE: To broil fish, place fish on the unheated rack of a broiler pan. Broil 4 inches from the heat for 8 to 12 minutes or until fish flakes easily with a fork, turning and brushing once with reserved marinade after 5 minutes.

Per serving: 248 cal., 10 g total fat (2 g sat. fat), 22 mg chol., 337 mg sodium, 2 g carbo., 0 g fiber, 34 g pro.

Pan-Seared Tilapia with Almond Browned Butter and Snow Peas

START TO FINISH: 20 minutes **MAKES:** 4 servings

- 3 cups snow pea pods, trimmed
- 4 4- to 5-ounce skinless fresh tilapia fillets
  Sea salt and freshly ground pepper
- 1 teaspoon all-purpose flour
- 1 tablespoon olive oil
- 2 tablespoons butter
- ¼ cup coarsely chopped almonds
- 1 tablespoon snipped fresh parsley

1. In a large saucepan bring lightly salted water to boiling. Add pea pods. Cook for 2 minutes. Drain and set aside.

2. Meanwhile, season one side of fish with salt and pepper; sprinkle with flour. Heat a large skillet over medium-high heat. When hot (a drop of water should sizzle or roll) remove from heat and add olive oil, tilting pan to coat with oil. Return pan to heat and add fish, floured side up (if necessary, cook fish half at a time). Cook fish for 4 to 5 minutes or until it is easy to remove with spatula. Gently turn fish and cook for 2 to 3 minutes more or until fish flakes easily when tested with a fork. Arrange peas on a serving platter; arrange fish on top of peas.

3. Reduce heat to medium. Add butter to skillet. When butter begins to melt, stir in almonds. Cook for 30 to 60 seconds or until butter is melted and nuts are lightly toasted (do not let butter burn). Spoon butter mixture over fish fillets. Sprinkle with parsley.

Per serving: 266 cal., 15 g total fat (5 g sat. fat), 71 mg chol., 210 mg sodium, 7 g carbo., 3 g fiber, 24 g pro.

Pecan-Cornmeal Fried Catfish

PREP: 20 minutes **COOK:** fry 4 minutes per batch
MAKES: 6 servings

1½ pounds fresh or frozen catfish fillets
¾ cup ground pecans or peanuts
⅔ cup yellow cornmeal
¾ teaspoon salt
¼ teaspoon ground black pepper
¼ teaspoon cayenne pepper
¼ cup milk
1 egg, beaten
  Cooking oil for deep-fat frying

1. Thaw fish, if frozen. Rinse fish; pat dry. Cut fish into
6 serving-size pieces, if necessary.

2. In a shallow dish combine ground pecans, cornmeal, salt, black
pepper, and cayenne pepper. In another shallow dish combine
milk and egg.

3. Dip each fish portion in milk mixture; coat with the
nut mixture.

4. Meanwhile, in a heavy large saucepan or deep fryer heat
2 inches of oil to 375°F. Fry fish in hot oil, 1 or 2 pieces at a time,
about 2 minutes on each side or until golden brown. Carefully
remove with a slotted spoon; drain on paper towels. Keep warm
in a 300°F oven while frying remaining fish.

Per serving: 397 cal., 28 g total fat (4 g sat. fat), 89 mg chol., 367 mg sodium,
15 g carbo., 2 g fiber, 21 g pro.

Nutty Fish and Roasted Sweet Potatoes

PREP: 30 minutes **BAKE:** 4 to 6 minutes per ½-inch thickness
MAKES: 6 servings

6 3- to 4-ounce fresh or frozen white fish fillets (such as tilapia,
  cod, orange roughy, or flounder)
  Nonstick cooking spray
½ cup all-purpose flour
2 eggs
2 tablespoons water
¾ cup finely chopped pecans
3 tablespoons ground flaxseeds
2 tablespoons packed brown sugar
¼ teaspoon salt

1. Thaw fish, if frozen. Rinse fish; pat dry with paper towels.
Measure thickness of fish fillets; set aside. Preheat the oven to 450°F.
Coat a large baking sheet with nonstick cooking spray; set aside.

2. Place flour in a shallow bowl. In another shallow bowl,
combine eggs and the water; beat with a fork. In a third shallow
bowl, combine pecans, flaxseeds, sugar, and salt.

3. Dip each fish fillet in flour, turning to coat both sides and
shaking off excess. Dip in egg mixture, then coat generously with
pecan mixture. Place fish fillets on the prepared baking sheet.
Bake until fish flakes easily when tested with a fork. Allow 4 to
6 minutes per ½-inch thickness.

Per serving: 273 cal., 14 g total fat (2 g sat. fat), 113 mg chol., 167 mg sodium,
15 g carbo., 3 g fiber, 22 g pro.

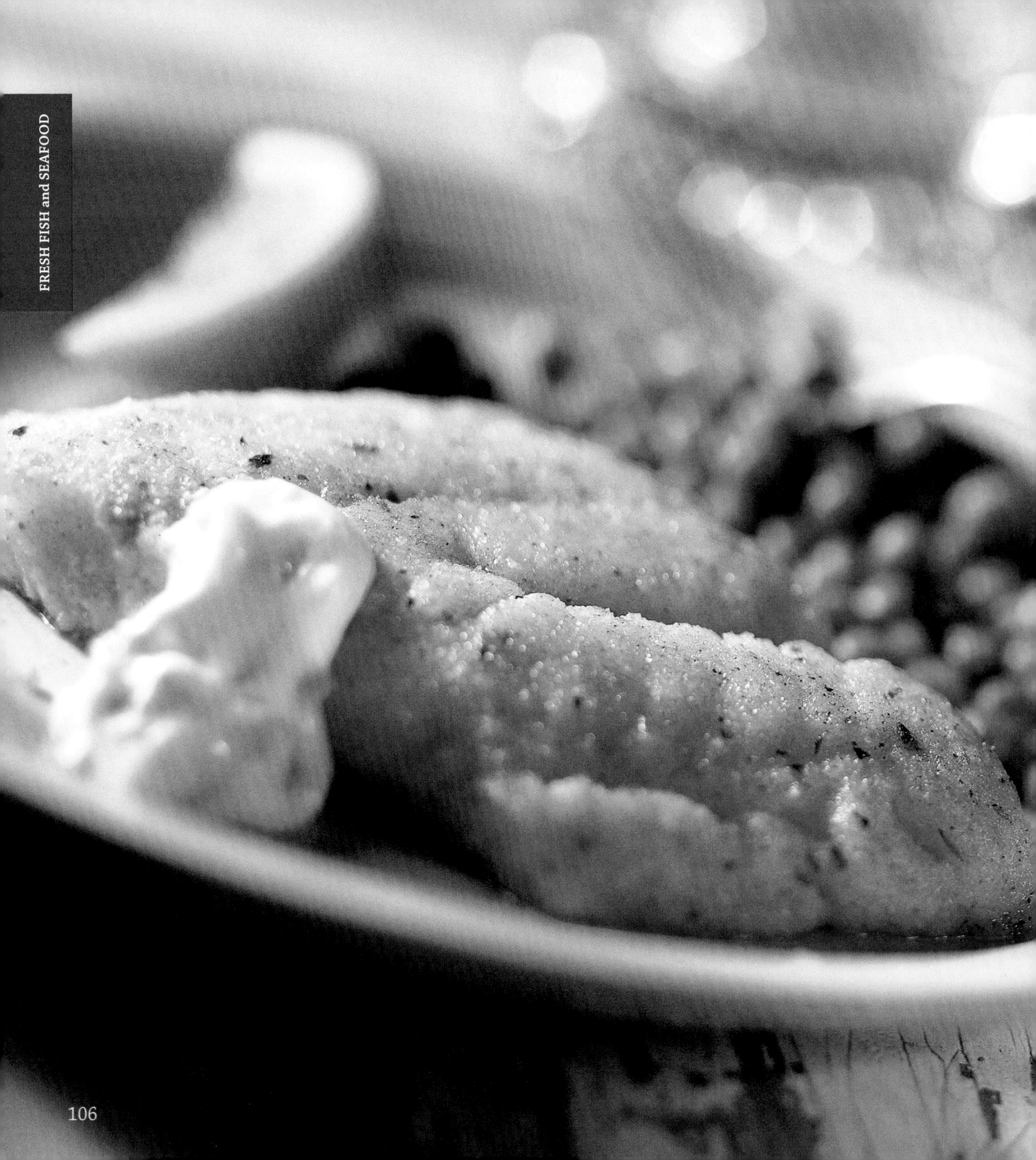

Fried Whitefish

START TO FINISH: 25 minutes **MAKES:** 4 servings

    1   cup all-purpose breading mix (about ¹/₂ of a 10-ounce package)
    1   cup packaged biscuit mix
    ¹/₃ cup grated Parmesan cheese
    1   tablespoon onion soup mix
    1¹/₂ teaspoons paprika
    1¹/₂ teaspoons dried Italian seasoning, crushed
    1¹/₂ teaspoons dried parsley flakes
    ¹/₂ teaspoon garlic powder
    1   to 1¹/₄ pounds fresh or frozen whitefish, haddock, or other
         firm-textured fish fillets
         Cooking oil for frying

1. Stir together the breading mix, biscuit mix, Parmesan cheese, onion soup mix, paprika, Italian seasoning, dried parsley, and garlic powder. Place half of the mixture in a shallow dish. (Place remaining mixture in a jar or self-sealing plastic bag. Cover or seal. Store in the refrigerator for up to 3 weeks. Stir or shake mixture before using.)

2. Thaw fish, if frozen. Rinse and pat dry. Cut into four pieces. Measure thickness of fish. Dip into breading mixture, turning to coat both sides.

3. In a large skillet heat ¹/₄ inch oil over medium heat. Add fish in a single layer. (If fillets have skin, fry skin side last.) Fry on one side until golden brown. Allow 3 to 4 minutes per side for ¹/₂-inch-thick fillets (5 to 6 minutes per side for 1-inch-thick fillets). Turn carefully. Fry until fish flakes easily when tested with a fork. Drain on paper towels. Keep warm in a 300°F oven while frying remaining fish.

Per serving: 352 cal., 17 g total fat (4 g sat. fat), 69 mg chol., 795 mg sodium, 21 g carbo., 0 g fiber, 25 g pro.

Oven-Fried Fish

PREP: 15 minutes **BAKE:** 4 minutes per ¹/₂-inch thickness
MAKES: 4 servings

    1   pound fresh or frozen skinless cod, orange roughy, or catfish fillets
    ¹/₄ cup milk
    ¹/₃ cup all-purpose flour
    ¹/₂ cup fine dry bread crumbs
    2   tablespoons grated Parmesan cheese
    ¹/₄ teaspoon lemon-pepper seasoning
    2   tablespoons butter, melted
         Lemon wedges (optional)

1. Preheat oven to 450°F. Thaw fish, if frozen. Rinse fish; pat dry with paper towels. If necessary, cut into four serving-size pieces. Measure the thickness of each piece. Place milk in a shallow dish. Place flour in another shallow dish. In a third shallow dish, combine bread crumbs, Parmesan cheese, and lemon-pepper seasoning. Add melted butter to bread crumb mixture; stir until well mixed.

2. Grease a shallow baking pan; set aside. Dip fish in the milk; coat with flour. Dip again in the milk; dip in the crumb mixture, turning to coat all sides. Place fish in a single layer in prepared baking pan. Bake, uncovered, for 4 to 6 minutes per ¹/₂-inch thickness or until fish flakes easily when tested with a fork. If desired, serve with lemon wedges.

Per serving: 254 cal., 9 g total fat (5 g sat. fat), 75 mg chol., 565 mg sodium, 15 g carbo., 1 g fiber, 26 g pro.

Pasta with Shrimp and Basil

START TO FINISH: 23 minutes **MAKES:** 4 servings

- 1 pound fresh or frozen peeled, deveined medium shrimp (1¹/₂ pounds medium shrimp in shell)
- 6 ounces dried spinach linguine, fettuccine, and/or fusilli pasta
- 2 teaspoons snipped fresh basil or tarragon or 1 teaspoon dried basil or tarragon, crushed
- 2 tablespoons butter

1. Thaw shrimp, if frozen. Cook pasta according to package directions. Drain and return pasta to pan. Meanwhile, in a large skillet cook shrimp and basil in butter over medium-high heat for 2 to 3 minutes or until shrimp are opaque, stirring frequently. Toss the shrimp with the hot pasta.

Per serving: 332 cal., 9 g total fat (4 g sat. fat), 189 mg chol., 231 mg sodium, 33 g carbo., 1 g fiber, 29 g pro.

Thai-Style Shrimp

START TO FINISH: 20 minutes MAKES: 4 servings

12 fresh or frozen large shrimp in shells
2 teaspoons cooking oil
1 small onion, coarsely chopped
2 teaspoons bottled minced garlic
2 to 3 tablespoons finely chopped fresh Thai or serrano chile peppers (see note, page 75)
2 medium cucumbers, halved lengthwise, seeded, and cut into 1/4-inch-thick slices
2 cups fresh pea pods, trimmed
2 tablespoons rice vinegar
2 teaspoons toasted sesame oil
1/4 cup chopped honey-roasted peanuts
1 tablespoon snipped cilantro

1. Thaw shrimp, if frozen. Peel and devein shrimp, leaving tails intact (if desired). Rinse shrimp; pat dry with paper towels. Set aside.

2. In a large nonstick skillet heat cooking oil over medium heat; cook onion, garlic, pepper, and cucumber for 7 minutes or until tender, stirring occasionally. Add shrimp; cook and stir, uncovered, for 3 minutes or until shrimp turn opaque. Stir in pea pods. Cook and stir for 1 minute more or until pea pods are crisp-tender.

3. Stir in vinegar and sesame oil. Serve immediately. Sprinkle with peanuts and snipped cilantro.

Per serving: 270 cal., 7 g total fat (1 g sat. fat), 129 mg chol., 134 mg sodium, 30 g carbo., 2 g fiber, 21 g pro.

109

Divine Crab Cakes

PREP: 15 minutes **COOK:** 6 minutes per batch
MAKES: 4 servings

 2 beaten eggs
³/₄ cup soft bread crumbs
¹/₃ cup mayonnaise or salad dressing
 I teaspoon dry mustard
 I teaspoon lemon juice
 I teaspoon Worcestershire sauce
¹/₂ teaspoon salt
¹/₄ teaspoon ground black pepper
¹/₈ teaspoon bottled hot pepper sauce (optional)
 I pound cooked crabmeat, finely flaked
¹/₃ cup fine dry bread crumbs
 2 tablespoons cooking oil

I. In a large bowl combine the eggs, soft bread crumbs, mayonnaise, mustard, lemon juice, Worcestershire sauce, salt, black pepper, and, if desired, hot pepper sauce. Stir in crabmeat; mix well. Shape mixture into eight ¹/₂-inch-thick patties.

2. Coat patties with the bread crumbs. In large skillet heat oil over medium heat. Cook crab cakes, four at a time, in hot oil about 3 minutes on each side or until golden brown. Keep warm while cooking remaining crab cakes. (Add additional oil to skillet, if necessary.)

Per serving (2 cakes): 399 cal., 27 g total fat (4 g sat. fat), 226 mg chol., 975 mg sodium, 10 g carbo., 0 g fiber, 28 g pro.

Crab Quiche

PREP: 10 minutes **BAKE:** 40 minutes **STAND:** 10 minutes
MAKES: 8 servings

- ½ of a 15-ounce package rolled refrigerated unbaked piecrust (1 crust)
- 3 tablespoons finely chopped green onion
- 1 tablespoon butter
- 3 eggs
- ½ pound cooked crabmeat (2 cups) or one 6- to 8-ounce package flake-style imitation crabmeat
- 1 cup half-and-half, light cream, or milk
- 3 tablespoons dry vermouth (optional)
- 1 tablespoon tomato paste
- 1 teaspoon salt
- ¼ teaspoon ground black pepper
- ½ cup shredded Swiss cheese (2 ounces)

1. Preheat oven to 450°F. Prepare piecrust and bake in a 9-inch pie plate as directed on package; set aside. Reduce oven temperature to 375°F. In a small skillet cook onion in hot butter until tender. Remove from heat.

2. In a medium bowl beat eggs slightly with a fork. Stir in crabmeat, half-and-half, vermouth (if using), tomato paste, salt, and pepper. Stir in onion mixture. Pour egg mixture into pastry shell. Sprinkle with shredded cheese.

3. Bake the quiche about 30 minutes or until a knife inserted near the center comes out clean. Let stand for 10 minutes before serving. Cut into wedges to serve.

TIP: You may want to cut the salt in the quiche filling to ½ teaspoon if using the imitation crabmeat (which is high in sodium).

Per serving: 279 cal., 18 g total fat (7 g sat. fat), 130 mg chol., 498 mg sodium, 16 g carbo., 1 g fiber, 13 g pro.

5 Heartwarming Soups and Stews

Mmmmm … there's nothing like a simmering hot pot of soup (or stew) when the weather gets frosty. These dishes will keep you warm until the spring thaw.

Beef Goulash Soup

PREP: 25 minutes **COOK:** 20 minutes **MAKES:** 4 servings

6 ounces boneless beef sirloin
1 teaspoon olive oil
1 medium onion, cut into thin wedges
2 cups water
1 14.5-ounce can no-salt-added tomatoes, undrained and cut up
1 14-ounce can beef broth
1/2 cup thinly sliced carrot
1 teaspoon unsweetened cocoa powder
1 clove garlic, minced
1 cup thinly sliced cabbage
1 ounce dried wide noodles (about 3/4 cup)
2 teaspoons paprika
1/4 cup fat-free dairy sour cream

1. Trim fat from meat. Cut meat into 1/2-inch pieces. In a large saucepan cook meat in hot oil over medium-high heat until meat is brown. Add onion wedges; cook and stir about 3 minutes or until onion is tender.

2. Stir in water, undrained tomatoes, beef broth, carrot, cocoa powder, and garlic. Bring to boiling; reduce heat. Simmer, uncovered, about 15 minutes or until meat is tender.

3. Stir in cabbage, noodles, and paprika. Simmer, uncovered, for 5 to 7 minutes more or until noodles are tender but still firm. Remove from heat. Stir in sour cream.

Per serving: 178 cal., 6 g total fat (2 g sat. fat), 34 mg chol., 400 mg sodium, 17 g carbo., 2 g fiber, 15 g pro.

Hearty Mushroom and Beef Soup

PREP: 20 minutes **COOK:** 1 hour 10 minutes **MAKES:** 4 servings

- 1 tablespoon cooking oil
- 1 pound boneless beef chuck, cut into 1/2-inch cubes
- 1 medium onion, chopped (1/2 cup)
- 3 cups beef broth
- 1/2 of a 28-ounce can (13/4 cups) crushed tomatoes
- 8 ounces fresh mushrooms, sliced
- 3/4 teaspoon dried oregano, crushed
- 3/4 teaspoon bottled minced garlic
- 1 bay leaf
- 1/2 cup sliced carrot
- 2 tablespoons cold water
- 4 teaspoons cornstarch
- 1 cup cooked rice
- 1/4 cup dry red wine (optional)
  Fresh rosemary sprigs or snipped parsley (optional)

1. In large saucepan or Dutch oven, heat oil over medium-high heat; add half of the meat. Cook and stir 2 to 3 minutes or until browned. Remove with slotted spoon. Repeat with remaining meat and the onion. Return all meat to pan. Stir in beef broth, crushed tomatoes, mushrooms, oregano, garlic, and bay leaf. Bring to boiling; reduce heat. Cover and simmer for 1 hour.

2. Add carrot. Return to boiling; reduce heat. Cover and simmer soup for 7 minutes. Combine cold water and cornstarch; add to pan along with rice. Cook and stir until slightly thickened. Add wine, if desired; heat for 2 minutes more. Discard bay leaf. Garnish with rosemary, if desired.

Per serving: 351 cal., 13 g total fat (4 g sat. fat), 82 mg chol., 914 mg sodium, 26 g carbo., 3 g fiber, 32 g pro.

Beef-Vegetable Soup

PREP: 35 minutes **COOK:** 2½ hours **MAKES:** 8 servings

- 3 pounds meaty beef shank crosscuts
- 2 tablespoons cooking oil
- 6 cups water
- 2 cups tomato juice
- 4 teaspoons instant beef bouillon granules
- 1 tablespoon Worcestershire sauce
- 1 teaspoon chili powder
- 2 bay leaves
- 2 medium carrots, diagonally sliced (1 cup)
- 2 medium stalks celery, sliced (1 cup)
- 1 large potato, peeled and cubed (1 cup)
- 1 cup coarsely chopped cabbage
- 1 small onion, coarsely chopped (⅓ cup)

1. In a 4-quart Dutch oven brown meat, half at a time, in the hot oil; drain off fat. Return all meat to pan. Stir in the water, tomato juice, beef bouillon granules, Worcestershire sauce, chili powder, and bay leaves. Bring to boiling; reduce heat. Cover and simmer for 2 hours. Remove beef crosscuts. Skim fat from broth.

2. When cool enough to handle, remove meat from bones; discard bones. Coarsely chop meat.

3. Stir chopped meat, carrots, celery, potato, cabbage, and onion into broth. Bring to boiling; reduce heat. Cover and simmer 30 to 45 minutes or until vegetables and beef are tender. Discard bay leaves.

Per serving: 185 cal., 5 g total fat (2 g sat. fat), 55 mg chol., 743 mg sodium, 9 g carbo., 2 g fiber, 26 g pro.

Barley Soup with Meatballs

PREP: 25 minutes **COOK:** 20 minutes **MAKES:** 6 to 8 servings

- 4 slices bacon or peppered bacon
- ¹/₂ cup chopped onion (1 medium)
- 2 cloves garlic, minced
- 1 1- to 1¹/₂-pound butternut or acorn squash, peeled and cut into ³/₄-inch pieces (about 4 cups)
- 2 medium carrots, cut into ³/₄-inch pieces
- 2 medium parsnips, cut into ³/₄-inch pieces
- 4 14-ounce cans reduced-sodium chicken broth or lower-sodium beef broth (about 7 cups)
- 1 cup apple juice or water
- 1 teaspoon dried Italian seasoning, dried thyme, or dried oregano, crushed
- 1 cup quick-cooking barley
- 24 frozen cooked meatballs, thawed (about ²/₃ of a 16-ounce package)
  Salt and ground black pepper

1. In a 4-quart Dutch oven cook bacon until crisp. Remove bacon from pan, reserving 1 tablespoon drippings in pan. Drain bacon on paper towels; set aside.

2. Cook onion and garlic in reserved drippings over medium heat until tender. Add squash, carrots, and parsnips; cook for 5 minutes more, stirring occasionally. Add broth, apple juice, and Italian seasoning. Bring to boiling; stir in barley. Reduce heat. Simmer, covered, for 10 to 15 minutes or until barley and vegetables are tender. Add meatballs; heat through. Season to taste with salt and pepper.

3. To serve, ladle into bowls. Crumble cooked bacon and sprinkle over individual servings.

MAKE-AHEAD DIRECTIONS: Prepare as above, except place cooked bacon in a resealable plastic bag. Quick chill the soup by placing Dutch oven in a sink filled with ice water for 10 minutes, stirring frequently. Transfer soup to a storage container. Cover and refrigerate soup and bacon up to 3 days. To serve, transfer soup to a 4-quart Dutch oven. Bring soup to boiling; stirring frequently. Serve as above. (Do not freeze the soup.)

Per serving: 402 cal., 13 g total fat (5 g sat. fat), 89 mg chol., 1,117 mg sodium, 47 g carbo., 7 g fiber, 23 g pro.

Hot and Sour Soup

START TO FINISH: 30 minutes **MAKES:** 4 servings

- 4 ounces fresh shiitake mushrooms, stemmed, with caps thinly sliced
- 1 teaspoon bottled minced garlic (2 cloves)
- 2 teaspoons peanut oil or cooking oil
- 2 14-ounce cans reduced-sodium chicken broth
- 2 tablespoons white vinegar or seasoned rice vinegar
- 2 tablespoons reduced-sodium soy sauce
- 1/2 teaspoon crushed red pepper
- 1 cup shredded cooked chicken (about 5 ounces)
- 2 cups packaged shredded cabbage with carrot (coleslaw mix) or shredded napa cabbage
- 2 tablespoons cold water
- 1 tablespoon cornstarch
- 1 teaspoon toasted sesame oil
   Carrot triangles (optional)

1. In a large saucepan cook mushrooms and garlic in hot oil over medium heat for 4 minutes, stirring occasionally. Stir in broth, vinegar, soy sauce, and red pepper; bring to boiling. Stir in chicken and coleslaw mix; reduce heat. Simmer, uncovered, for 5 minutes.

2. In a small bowl combine the cold water and cornstarch. Stir into soup; simmer about 2 minutes or until slightly thickened. Remove from heat; stir in sesame oil. If desired, garnish individual servings with carrot triangles.

Per serving: 157 cal., 7 g total fat (1 g sat. fat), 34 mg chol., 889 mg sodium, 9 g carbo., 1 g fiber, 15 g pro.

Tortellini Chicken Soup

START TO FINISH: 25 minutes **MAKES:** 4 servings

-    Nonstick cooking spray
- 12 ounces skinless, boneless chicken breast halves, cut into 1/2-inch cubes
- 6 cups reduced-sodium chicken broth
- 1/2 cup sliced leek or chopped onion
- 1 tablespoon grated fresh ginger
- 1/4 teaspoon saffron threads, slightly crushed (optional)
- 1 9-ounce package refrigerated herb chicken tortellini or vegetable ravioli
- 1/2 cup fresh baby spinach leaves or shredded fresh spinach

1. Lightly coat an unheated large saucepan with cooking spray. Heat over medium-high heat. Add chicken; cook and stir for 3 minutes. Carefully add broth, leek, ginger, and, if desired, saffron.

2. Bring to boiling. Add tortellini or ravioli. Return to boiling; reduce heat. Simmer, uncovered, for 5 to 9 minutes or until tortellini or ravioli is tender, stirring occasionally. Remove from heat. Top individual servings with spinach.

Per serving: 222 cal., 3 g total fat (0 g sat. fat), 59 mg chol., 1221 mg sodium, 21 g carbo., 3 g fiber, 29 g pro.

Turkey Tortilla Soup

START TO FINISH: 20 minutes **MAKES:** 4 servings

3 6-inch corn tortillas, cut in strips
2 tablespoons cooking oil
1 cup purchased red or green salsa
2 14-ounce cans reduced sodium chicken broth
2 cups cubed cooked turkey (12 ounces)
1 large zucchini, coarsely chopped
   Lime wedges (optional)
   Sour cream and cilantro (optional)

1. In a large skillet cook tortilla strips in hot oil until crisp; remove with slotted spoon and drain on paper towels.

2. In a large saucepan combine salsa and chicken broth; bring to boiling over medium-high heat. Add turkey and zucchini; heat through. Serve in bowls topped with tortilla strips. If desired, garnish with lime wedges and cilantro.

Per serving: 262 cal., 11 g total fat (2 g sat. fat), 53 mg chol., 920 mg sodium, 16 g carbo., 3 g fiber, 26 g pro.

Turkey and Rice Soup

START TO FINISH: 25 minutes MAKES: 6 servings

2 14-ounce cans reduced-sodium chicken broth
1½ cups water
1 teaspoon snipped fresh rosemary or ¼ teaspoon dried
   rosemary, crushed
¼ teaspoon black pepper
½ cup thinly sliced carrot (1 medium)
½ cup thinly sliced celery (1 stalk)
⅓ cup chopped onion (1 small)
1 cup quick-cooking rice
½ cup loose-pack frozen cut green beans
2 cups chopped cooked turkey or chicken (about 10 ounces)
1 14.5-ounce can diced tomatoes, undrained
   Fresh rosemary sprigs (optional)

1. In a large saucepan or Dutch oven combine broth, the water, rosemary, and pepper. Add carrot, celery, and onion. Bring to boiling.

2. Stir in uncooked rice and green beans. Return to boiling; reduce heat. Simmer, covered, for 10 to 12 minutes or until vegetables are tender. Stir in turkey or chicken and undrained tomatoes; heat through. If desired, garnish with rosemary sprigs.

Per serving: 177 cal., 2 g total fat (1 g sat. fat), 35 mg chol., 500 mg sodium, 20 g carbo., 1 g fiber, 17 g pro.

Quick-Fix Turkey and Rice Soup

PREP: 15 minutes COOK: 10 minutes MAKES: 6 servings

- 4 cups chicken broth
- 1 cup water
- 1 teaspoon snipped fresh rosemary or ¼ teaspoon dried rosemary, crushed
- ¼ teaspoon ground black pepper
- 2 cups frozen mixed vegetables
- 1 cup instant white rice
- 2 cups chopped cooked turkey or chicken
- 1 14.5-ounce can tomatoes, cut up (undrained)

1. In a large saucepan or Dutch oven combine chicken broth, water, rosemary, and pepper. Bring to boiling. Stir in mixed vegetables and rice.

2. Return to boiling; reduce heat. Cover and simmer for 10 to 15 minutes or until vegetables and rice are tender. Stir in turkey or chicken and undrained tomatoes. Heat through.

Per serving: 209 cal., 4 g total fat (1 g sat. fat), 36 mg chol., 699 mg sodium, 24 g carbo., 20 g pro.

Turkey Sausage and Bean Soup

PREP: 20 minutes COOK: 10 minutes MAKES: 4 servings

   4   cups chicken broth
   2   15-ounce cans white kidney beans (cannellini), great northern
       beans, or red kidney beans, rinsed and drained
 ¹/₂   pound cooked turkey kielbasa, halved lengthwise and cut
       into ¹/₂-inch-thick pieces
   I   medium onion, chopped (¹/₂ cup)
   I   teaspoon dried basil, crushed
 ¹/₄   teaspoon coarsely ground black pepper
 ¹/₂   teaspoon bottled minced garlic or I clove garlic, minced,
       or ¹/₈ teaspoon garlic powder
   3   cups packaged fresh spinach

I. In a large saucepan or Dutch oven combine chicken broth, beans, kielbasa, onion, basil, pepper, and garlic. Bring to boiling; reduce heat. Cover and simmer for 10 to 15 minutes or until onion is tender.

2. Meanwhile, remove stems from spinach. Stack the leaves one on top of the other and cut into 1-inch-wide strips. Just before serving, stir spinach into soup.

Per serving: 257 cal., 6 g total fat (2 g sat. fat), 39 mg chol., 1,620 mg sodium, 35 g carbo., II g fiber, 28 g pro.

Curried Spinach Soup

START TO FINISH: 30 minutes MAKES: 8 servings

- 1 large potato, peeled and chopped
- 1/2 cup sliced green onions (4)
- 6 tablespoons butter
- 1 pound fresh spinach, washed and stems trimmed (12 cups)
- 1/3 cup all-purpose flour
- 2 teaspoons curry powder
- 4 cups chicken broth
- 1 tablespoon lemon juice
- 1 8-ounce carton dairy sour cream
  Croutons (optional)

1. In a large saucepan cook potato and green onion in 2 tablespoons of the butter over medium heat about 10 minutes or until potatoes are tender. Slowly add the spinach, one-fifth at a time, stirring just until spinach is limp and dark green after each addition. In a food processor or blender process or blend the spinach mixture, half at a time, until smooth.

2. In the same saucepan melt remaining 4 tablespoons butter over medium heat. Stir in flour and curry powder; cook and stir for 2 minutes. Slowly add broth, whisking until combined. Stir in spinach mixture and lemon juice. Cook and stir over medium heat until mixture is slightly thickened and bubbly; cook and stir 1 minute more. In a medium bowl stir about 1 cup of the the hot mixture into sour cream. Return mixture to saucepan. Heat through but do not boil. Top with croutons, if desired.

Per serving: 192 cal., 15 g total fat (9 g sat. fat), 37 mg chol., 488 mg sodium, 10 g carbo., 6 g fiber, 5 g pro.

Hash Brown Potato and Sausage Chowder

START TO FINISH: 20 minutes **MAKES:** 5 servings

1	20-ounce package refrigerated shredded hash brown potatoes
1	14-ounce can reduced-sodium chicken broth
2	cups loose-pack frozen whole kernel corn
2	cups milk
12	ounces cooked smoked sausage, halved lengthwise and sliced
1/3	cup sliced green onions (3)
1/4	teaspoon ground black pepper
	Salt
	Green or red bottled hot pepper sauce

1. In a 4-quart Dutch oven or saucepan combine potatoes, broth, and corn. Bring just to boiling; reduce heat. Cover and simmer about 10 minutes or just until potatoes are tender, stirring occasionally.

2. Using a potato masher, slightly mash potatoes. Stir in milk, sausage, green onions, and black pepper; heat through. Season to taste with salt and hot pepper sauce.

TIP: For a lower-fat soup, substitute light smoked sausage for the regular sausage and fat-free milk for the regular milk.

Per serving: 444 cal., 23 g total fat (11 g sat. fat), 38 mg chol., 979 mg sodium, 45 g carbo., 3 g fiber, 17 g pro.

Cheesy Chicken Chowder

PREP: 25 minutes **COOK:** 15 minutes **MAKES:** 16 servings

- 1 large onion, chopped (1 cup)
- 1 cup thinly sliced celery
- 2 cloves garlic, minced
- 1 tablespoon cooking oil
- 1½ pounds skinless, boneless chicken breast halves, cut into bite-size pieces
- 1 32-ounce package frozen diced hash-brown potatoes
- 2 14-ounce cans chicken broth
- 1 2.64-ounce envelope country gravy mix
- 2 cups milk
- 1 8-ounce package process cheese spread, cut into chunks
- 1 16-ounce jar chunky salsa
- 1 4.5-ounce can diced green chili peppers
  Corn chips

1. In a 6-quart Dutch oven cook and stir onion, celery and garlic in hot oil over medium heat about 5 minutes or until onion is tender. Add chicken; cook and stir about 3 minutes or until no longer pink. Add potatoes and broth. Bring to boiling; reduce heat. Simmer, covered, for 12 to 15 minutes or until potatoes are tender, stirring occasionally.

2. Meanwhile, in a medium bowl dissolve gravy mix in milk. Stir milk mixture into soup mixture. Stir in cheese, salsa and green chilies; reduce heat to low. Cook and stir until cheese is melted. Serve with corn chips.

Per serving: 303 cal., 15 g total fat (5 g sat. fat), 35 mg chol., 857 mg sodium, 26 g carbo., 2 g fiber, 16 g pro.

Chicken and Potato Chowder

START TO FINISH: 40 minutes **MAKES:** 4 servings

- ½ cup chopped onion
- 1 tablespoon butter
- 2 cups fresh or frozen whole kernel corn
- 1½ cups reduced-sodium chicken broth
- 1½ cups chopped, peeled potato
- 1 4-ounce can diced green chile peppers, drained
- ¼ teaspoon coarsely ground black pepper
- 2 cups milk
- 2 tablespoons all-purpose flour
- 5 ounces cooked chicken, cut into thin strips (1 cup)
- 2 tablespoons snipped fresh cilantro or 2 teaspoons snipped fresh oregano

1. In a large saucepan cook onion in hot butter for 3 to 4 minutes or until tender. Add corn, chicken broth, potato, chile peppers, and black pepper. Bring to boiling; reduce heat. Cover and simmer about 15 minutes or until potatoes are tender, stirring occasionally.

2. In a screw-top jar combine milk and flour; cover and shake well. Add to potato mixture. Cook and stir until thickened and bubbly. Add chicken and cilantro. Heat through.

Per serving: 311 cal., 9 g total fat (4 g sat. fat), 49 mg chol., 446 mg sodium, 40 g carbo., 4 g fiber, 20 g pro.

Turkey and Sweet Potato Chowder

PREP: 20 minutes **COOK:** 24 minutes **MAKES:** 5 servings

- 1 large potato, peeled if desired and chopped (about 1½ cups)
- 1 14-ounce can reduced-sodium chicken broth
- 2 small ears frozen corn-on-the-cob, thawed, or 1 cup loose-pack frozen whole kernel corn
- 12 ounces cooked turkey breast, cut into ½-inch cubes (about 2¼ cups)
- 1½ cups fat-free milk
- 1 large sweet potato, peeled and cut into ¾-inch cubes (about 1½ cups)
- ⅛ to ¼ teaspoon ground black pepper
- ¼ cup coarsely snipped fresh flat-leaf parsley

1. In a 3-quart saucepan combine chopped potato and broth. Bring to boiling; reduce heat. Simmer, uncovered, about 12 minutes or until potato is tender, stirring occasionally. Remove from heat. Do not drain. Using a potato masher, mash potato until mixture is thickened and nearly smooth.

2. If using corn-on-the-cob, cut the kernels from one of the ears of corn. Carefully cut the second ear of corn crosswise into ½-inch-thick slices.

3. Stir corn, turkey, milk, sweet potato, and pepper into potato mixture in saucepan. Bring to boiling; reduce heat. Cover and cook for 12 to 15 minutes or until the sweet potato is tender.

4. To serve, ladle chowder into bowls. Sprinkle with parsley.

Per serving: 216 cal., 1 g total fat (0 g sat. fat), 44 mg chol., 271 mg sodium, 29 g carbo., 4 g fiber, 23 g pro.

Smoked Salmon Chowder

PREP: 15 minutes COOK: 25 minutes MAKES: 6 servings

¼ cup butter

2 cups sliced leeks

I clove garlic, minced

2 tablespoons all-purpose flour

3 cups fish stock or vegetable broth

1½ pounds Yukon gold potatoes, peeled and cut into
¼-inch cubes (3 cups)

½ teaspoon salt

¾ pound smoked salmon, skin and bones removed
and cut into bite-size pieces

¾ cup whipping cream

Sliced leeks (optional)

Ground black pepper

I. In a 4- to 5-quart Dutch oven melt butter over medium heat. Add the 2 cups leeks and garlic; cook and stir for 5 minutes or until soft. Stir in flour; cook and stir for 2 minutes more.

2. Gradually whisk the stock into the flour mixture in Dutch oven until smooth. Add potatoes and salt. Bring to boiling, stirring often. Reduce heat. Simmer, covered, for 10 to 15 minutes or just until potatoes are tender. Stir in salmon and cream. Heat through. If desired, garnish each serving with additional sliced leeks. Sprinkle with pepper.

Per serving: 370 cal., 23 g total fat (I3 g sat. fat), 75 mg chol., 903 mg sodium, 25 g carbo., 3 g fiber, I7 g pro.

Seafood and Corn Chowder

PREP: 15 minutes COOK: 20 minutes MAKES: 4 to 5 servings

- 1 14-ounce can chicken broth
- 1 cup sliced celery (2 stalks)
- 1 cup chopped onion (1 large)
- 1/2 cup sliced carrot (1 medium)
- 1 14.75-ounce can cream-style corn
- 1 cup whipping cream
- 1/2 teaspoon snipped fresh thyme or 1/4 teaspoon dried thyme, crushed
- 1/8 teaspoon ground black pepper
   Few dashes bottled hot pepper sauce
- 10 to 12 ounces cooked or canned lump crabmeat and/or peeled, deveined, cooked shrimp
   Fresh thyme sprigs (optional)
   Assorted crackers (optional)

1. In a medium saucepan combine broth, celery, onion, and carrot. Bring to boiling; reduce heat. Simmer, covered, about 20 minutes or until vegetables are tender. Cool slightly.

2. Transfer half of the broth mixture to a blender or food processor. Cover and blend or process until smooth. Repeat with remaining cooked mixture. Return mixture to saucepan. Stir in corn, whipping cream, thyme, pepper, and hot pepper sauce. Bring to boiling; reduce heat. Stir in crabmeat and/or shrimp; heat through. If desired, garnish each serving with fresh thyme and serve with assorted crackers.

Per serving: 388 cal., 24 g total fat (14 g sat. fat), 154 mg chol., 948 mg sodium, 27 g carbo., 3 g fiber, 18 g pro.

Cheesy Cauliflower Chowder

PREP: 20 minutes COOK: 10 minutes MAKES: 6 servings

- 1 large onion, chopped
- 2 tablespoons butter
- 4 cups chicken broth
- 2 cups chopped peeled Yukon gold or russet potato
- 2 1/2 cups cauliflower florets
- 1 cup half-and-half, light cream, or milk
- 2 tablespoons all-purpose flour
- 2 1/2 cups shredded Jarlsberg or Swiss cheese (10 ounces)
   Salt and ground black pepper
- 3 slices dark rye or pumpernickel bread, halved crosswise (optional)
- 1/2 cup shredded Jarlsberg or Swiss cheese (2 ounces) (optional)
- 2 tablespoons snipped fresh flat-leaf parsley (optional)

1. In large saucepan or Dutch oven, cook onion in hot butter until tender. Add chicken broth and potato. Bring to boiling; reduce heat. Cover and simmer for 6 minutes. Add cauliflower. Return to boiling; reduce heat. Cover and simmer for 4 to 6 minutes more or until vegetables are tender.

2. In small bowl whisk half-and-half into flour until smooth. Add to potato mixture. Cook and stir until thickened and bubbly. Reduce heat to low. Stir in the 2 1/2 cups cheese until melted. Do not boil. Season to taste with salt and ground black pepper.

3. Meanwhile, if using bread, preheat oven to 350°F. If desired, trim crusts from bread. Place bread on baking sheet. Bake about 3 minutes or until crisp on top. Turn bread; sprinkle with the 1/2 cup cheese and parsley. Bake about 5 minutes more or until cheese is melted.

4. Ladle potato mixture into soup bowls. Top each serving with cheese-topped bread.

Per serving: 267 cal., 17 g total fat (12 g sat. fat), 58 mg chol., 533 mg sodium, 14 g carbo., 2 g fiber, 15 g pro.

Pumpkin Bisque

START TO FINISH: 35 minutes **MAKES:** 8 small servings

- 1 medium onion, coarsely chopped
- 2 tablespoons butter
- 3 cups canned pumpkin
- 2 14-ounce cans chicken broth
- 2 tablespoons packed brown sugar
- 1/4 teaspoon ground nutmeg
- 1/4 teaspoon freshly ground black pepper
- 2 bay leaves
- 1 cup whipping cream
- 1 cup finely chopped cooked smoked ham
- 1 tablespoon cooking oil

1. In a 4-quart oven Dutch oven cook onion in hot butter until tender. Stir in pumpkin, broth, brown sugar, nutmeg, pepper, and bay leaves. Bring to boiling; reduce heat. Cover and simmer for 10 minutes. Remove soup from heat. Discard bay leaves. Stir in whipping cream.

2. Transfer about one-third of the mixture to a food processor or blender. Cover and process or blend until smooth. Repeat with remaining mixture, one-third at a time. Return all pumpkin mixture to the Dutch oven. Heat through.

3. Meanwhile, in a medium skillet, cook the finely chopped ham in hot oil over medium heat about 10 minutes or until ham is crisp. Drain off fat. To serve, sprinkle the crisp ham over individual servings of soup.

Per serving: 237 cal., 18 g total fat (10 g sat. fat), 60 mg chol., 711 mg sodium, 13 g carbo., 3 g fiber, 7 g pro.

Mushroom-Tomato Bisque

PREP: 20 minutes COOK: 40 minutes MAKES: 8 small servings

1 cup sliced leeks or chopped onion
1 cup sliced celery
4 cloves garlic, minced
3 tablespoons butter
3 cups sliced fresh shiitake or other mushrooms
2 14.5-ounce cans tomatoes, undrained and cut up
3 cups chicken broth or vegetable broth
1/2 cup whipping cream
2 tablespoons snipped fresh dill or 2 teaspoons dried dillweed
1/8 teaspoon ground black pepper
1 cup sliced fresh shiitake or other mushrooms
2 tablespoons butter
Fresh dill (optional)

1. Place leeks or onion, celery, and garlic in a large saucepan or Dutch oven. Add the 3 tablespoons butter and cook until tender. Add the 3 cups mushrooms and cook about 5 minutes more or until mushrooms are tender.

2. Stir in tomatoes, broth, whipping cream, dill, and pepper. Bring to boiling; reduce heat. Simmer, covered, for 30 minutes. Cool mixture slightly.

3. In a blender or food processor pour one-fourth of the tomato mixture. Cover and blend or process until smooth. Repeat with remaining tomato mixture. Return all tomato mixture to saucepan and heat through.

4. Meanwhile, in a small skillet place the 1 cup mushrooms and 2 tablespoons butter; cook until tender.

5. To serve, ladle bisque into serving bowls. Garnish with cooked mushrooms and, if desired, fresh dill.

Per serving: 117 cal., 14 g total fat (8 g sat. fat), 40 mg chol., 507 mg sodium, 9 g carbo., 2 g fiber, 5 g pro.

133

Hurry-Up Beef-Vegetable Stew

START TO FINISH: 20 minutes MAKES: 5 servings

- 2 cups water
- 1 10.75-ounce can condensed golden mushroom soup
- 1 10.75-ounce can condensed tomato soup
- 1/2 cup dry red wine or beef broth
- 2 cups chopped cooked roast beef
- 1 16-ounce package frozen sugar snap stir-fry vegetables or one 16-ounce package frozen cut broccoli
- 1/2 teaspoon dried thyme, crushed

1. In a 4-quart Dutch oven combine the water, mushroom soup, tomato soup, and wine. Stir in beef, frozen vegetables, and thyme. Cook over medium heat until bubbly, stirring frequently. Continue cooking, uncovered, for 4 to 5 minutes or until vegetables are crisp-tender, stirring occasionally.

Per serving: 231 cal., 4 g total fat (1 g sat. fat), 42 mg chol., 906 mg sodium, 21 g carbo., 4 g fiber, 20 g pro.

Summer Stew

START TO FINISH: 20 minutes **MAKES:** 4 servings

- 1 17-ounce package refrigerated cooked beef roast au jus
- 1 8-ounce package peeled fresh baby carrots, sliced
- 3½ cups water
- ½ of a 16-ounce package refrigerated rosemary-and-roasted garlic-seasoned, diced red-skinned potatoes (about 2 cups)
- 1 14.5-ounce can diced fire-roasted tomatoes with garlic
- 2 tablespoons snipped fresh oregano
  - Salt and freshly ground black pepper

l. Pour juices from beef roast into large saucepan; set meat aside. Add carrots and 1 cup water to saucepan; bring to boiling. Reduce heat and simmer, covered, 3 minutes. Add remaining water, potatoes, tomatoes, and 1 tablespoon of the oregano. Return to boiling; cover. Simmer 3 minutes or until vegetables are tender. Break beef into bite-size pieces and add to stew; heat through. Season with salt.

2. Spoon into shallow bowls; top with pepper and remaining oregano.

Per serving: 253 cal., 9 g total fat (4 g sat. fat), 64 mg chol., 948 mg sodium, 20 g carbo., 3 g fiber, 25 g pro.

Caribbean-Style Pork Stew

START TO FINISH: 30 minutes **MAKES:** 6 servings

- 1 15-ounce can black beans, rinsed and drained
- 1 14-ounce can beef broth or 1³/₄ cups homemade beef broth
- 1³/₄ cups water
- 12 ounces cooked lean boneless pork, cut into thin bite-size strips
- 3 plantains, peeled and cubed
- 1 cup chopped tomatoes
- ¹/₂ of a 16-ounce package (2 cups) frozen pepper stir-fry vegetables
- 1 tablespoon grated fresh ginger
- 1 teaspoon ground cumin
- ¹/₄ teaspoon crushed red pepper
- ¹/₄ teaspoon salt
- 3 cups hot cooked rice
   Crushed red pepper (optional)
   Fresh pineapple slices (optional)

1. In a 4-quart Dutch oven combine beans, broth, and water; bring to boiling. Add pork, plantains, and tomatoes. Stir in frozen vegetables, ginger, cumin, the ¹/₄ teaspoon crushed red pepper, and salt. Return to boiling; reduce heat. Simmer, covered, about 10 minutes or until plantains are tender.

2. Serve with rice. If desired, sprinkle each serving with additional crushed red pepper and garnish with pineapple.

Per serving: 367 cal., 5 g total fat (1 g sat. fat), 32 mg chol., 555 mg sodium, 64 g carbo., 7 g fiber, 22 g pro.

Peruvian Chicken Ragout

PREP: 20 minutes **COOK:** 25 minutes **MAKES:** 6 servings

- 1 pound skinless, boneless chicken thighs, cut into 1-inch pieces
- 2 tablespoons all-purpose flour
- 1 teaspoon chili powder
- 1/2 teaspoon salt
- 1/2 teaspoon ground black pepper
- 1 medium onion, chopped (1/2 cup)
- 1 clove garlic, minced
- 1 tablespoon cooking oil
- 1 28-ounce can diced tomatoes, undrained
- 1 14-ounce can chicken broth
- 1 medium potato, peeled and diced (1/2 cup)
- 1 cup frozen whole kernel corn
- 1/2 cup quinoa
- 2 cups packed fresh spinach leaves
  Finely shredded lemon peel (set aside)
- 2 tablespoons lemon juice

1. Place chicken, flour, chili powder, salt, and pepper in a plastic bag. Seal bag and shake to coat.

2. In a 4- to 6-quart Dutch oven cook chicken mixture, onion, and garlic in hot oil over medium heat until browned. Add undrained tomatoes, broth, potato, corn, and quinoa. Bring to boiling; reduce heat. Simmer, covered, for 15 to 20 minutes or until potatoes and quinoa are tender.

3. Stir in spinach and lemon juice. Garnish each serving with shredded lemon peel.

Per serving: 262 cal., 7 g total fat (1 g sat. fat), 63 mg chol., 761 mg sodium, 30 g carbo., 4 g fiber, 20 g pro.

Herb and Pepper Lentil Stew

PREP: 10 minutes **COOK:** 28 minutes **MAKES:** 4 servings

- 1 tablespoon cooking oil
- 2 medium onions, quartered
- 1 medium green sweet pepper, cut into ½-inch rings
- 1 tablespoon snipped fresh thyme or 1 teaspoon dried thyme, crushed
- ¼ teaspoon crushed red pepper
- 5 cups water
- 1¼ cups dry red (Egyptian) lentils,* rinsed and drained
- 1½ teaspoons salt
- 4 sprigs fresh thyme (optional)
  Flatbread (optional)

1. In a Dutch oven heat oil over medium-high heat for 30 seconds. Add onion quarters. Cook about 8 minutes or until browned, stirring occasionally.

2. Add green pepper, thyme, and crushed red pepper. Cook and stir 2 minutes. Remove from heat. Add water, 1 cup of lentils, and salt. Return to heat. Bring to boiling; reduce heat. Simmer, uncovered, for 15 minutes.

3. Add remaining lentils. Cook, uncovered, for 3 to 5 minutes more or until lentils are tender.

4. To serve, ladle stew into bowls. If desired, top with fresh thyme sprigs and serve with flatbread.

*NOTE: Brown or green lentils may be substituted for the red lentils. Prepare recipe as directed, except add all the lentils with water and salt. Bring to boiling; reduce heat. Simmer, covered, 25 minutes. Uncover. Simmer for 5 minutes more.

Per serving: 246 cal., 4 g total fat (1 g sat. fat), 0 mg chol., 902 mg sodium, 39 g carbo., 10 g fiber, 15 g pro.

Veal Stew with Polenta

START TO FINISH: 40 minutes MAKES: 4 servings

    I pound boneless veal round steak or lean boneless pork
    2 tablespoons olive oil
    I medium onion, cut into thin wedges
    I medium green or red sweet pepper, seeded and coarsely chopped
    2 cloves garlic, minced
    I 14.5-ounce can diced tomatoes, undrained
    ¼ cup dry red wine or water
    I teaspoon instant chicken bouillon granules
    I teaspoon dried Italian seasoning, crushed
    ½ teaspoon salt
    2¾ cups water
    ¼ teaspoon salt
    ¾ cup quick-cooking polenta mix
    2 cups torn fresh spinach

I. Trim fat from veal. Cut meat into ¹/₂-inch pieces. In a large saucepan heat 1 tablespoon of the oil over medium heat. Cook meat, half at a time, in hot oil until brown, stirring occasionally. Remove meat and drain; set aside. Add remaining 1 tablespoon oil to the same pan. Add onion, sweet pepper, and garlic; cook for 5 to 8 minutes or just until vegetables are tender, stirring occasionally. Add drained meat, undrained tomatoes, wine, bouillon granules, Italian seasoning, and the ¹/₂ teaspoon salt. Bring to boiling; reduce heat. Cover and simmer for 10 minutes.

2. Meanwhile, in a 2-quart saucepan heat the water and the ¹/₄ teaspoon salt to boiling. Stir in polenta mix. Cook, stirring frequently, for 5 minutes.

3. Stir spinach into veal mixture. To serve, divide polenta among four shallow soup bowls. Top with veal mixture.

Per serving: 370 cal., II g total fat (2 g sat. fat), 9I mg chol., 1,I80 mg sodium, 33 g carbo., 4 g fiber, 30 g pro.

Texas Bowls O' Red Chili

PREP: 30 minutes **COOK:** 1½ hours **MAKES:** 6 servings

    3 pounds boneless beef chuck roast, cut into ½-inch cubes
    1 teaspoon salt
    ½ teaspoon freshly ground black pepper
    1 tablespoon cooking oil
    4 cups chopped onions
    3 tablespoons chili powder
    3 tablespoons yellow cornmeal
    6 cloves garlic, minced
    1 tablespoon ground cumin
    2 teaspoons dried oregano, crushed
    ¼ teaspoon cayenne pepper
    1 14-ounce can beef broth or 1¾ cups homemade beef broth
 1¼ cups water
    1 tablespoon packed brown sugar
       Chopped onion (optional)

1. Sprinkle beef with ½ teaspoon of the salt and ¼ teaspoon of the black pepper. In a 4-quart Dutch oven heat oil. Add one-third of the beef; cook until brown. Using a slotted spoon, remove beef, reserving drippings in pan. Repeat with remaining beef, cooking one-third at a time, and adding more oil, if necessary.

2. Add the 4 cups chopped onions to drippings; cook over medium-high heat about 5 minutes or until tender. Stir in chili powder, cornmeal, garlic, cumin, oregano, and cayenne pepper; cook for 30 seconds. Stir in the beef, remaining ½ teaspoon salt, remaining ¼ teaspoon pepper, broth, water, and brown sugar. Bring to boiling; reduce heat. Simmer, covered, for 1½ to 2 hours or until meat is tender. If desired, top each serving with additional chopped onion.

Per serving: 448 cal., 17 g total fat (5 g sat. fat), 107 mg chol., 812 mg sodium, 19 g carbo., 4 g fiber, 53 g pro.

Chipotle Chili with Hominy and Beans

START TO FINISH: 30 minutes **MAKES:** 6 servings

Nonstick cooking spray
8 ounces extra-lean ground beef or uncooked ground chicken breast or turkey breast
1 large onion, chopped (1 cup)
1½ teaspoons ground cumin
½ teaspoon dried oregano, crushed
1 to 2 teaspoons chopped canned chipotle chile peppers in adobo sauce
2 14.5-ounce cans no-salt-added stewed tomatoes, undrained
1 15-ounce can red beans, rinsed and drained
1 15-ounce can yellow hominy, rinsed and drained
1 small green or red sweet pepper, chopped
½ cup water
6 tablespoons shredded cheddar cheese (optional)

1. Lightly coat an unheated large saucepan with cooking spray. Preheat over medium heat. Add beef and onion; cook until meat is brown. If necessary, drain off fat.

2. Stir in cumin and oregano; cook for 1 minute more. Add chipotle peppers, undrained tomatoes, drained beans, drained hominy, sweet pepper, and the water. Bring to boiling; reduce heat. Cover and simmer for 5 minutes. If desired, sprinkle each serving with cheese.

Per serving: 257 cal., 7 g total fat (3 g sat. fat), 26 mg chol., 477 mg sodium, 35 g carbo., 9 g fiber, 13 g pro.

Chunky Beer-Pork Chili

START TO FINISH: 30 minutes **MAKES:** 4 servings

- 12 ounces pork tenderloin
- 2 teaspoons chili powder
- 2 teaspoons ground cumin
- 1 small onion, chopped
- 2 teaspoons bottled minced garlic
- 1 tablespoon cooking oil
- 1 yellow or red sweet pepper, cut into 1/2-inch pieces
- 1 cup beer or beef broth
- 1/2 cup bottled picante sauce or salsa
- 1 to 2 tablespoons finely chopped canned chipotle chile pepper in adobo sauce
- 1 15- to 16-ounce can small red beans or pinto beans, rinsed and drained
- 1/2 cup dairy sour cream
  Fresh cilantro or flat-leaf parsley sprigs (optional)

1. Trim fat from meat. Cut meat into 3/4-inch pieces; transfer to medium bowl. Add chili powder and cumin; toss gently to coat. Set aside.

2. In a large saucepan, cook onion and garlic in hot oil over medium-high heat about 3 minutes or until tender. Add meat. Cook and stir until meat is brown.

3. Stir in sweet pepper, beer, picante sauce, and chipotle chile pepper. Bring to boiling; reduce heat. Cover and simmer about 5 minutes or until pork is tender. Stir in beans; heat through.

4. Top each serving with sour cream. If desired, garnish with cilantro.

Per serving: 328 cal., 11 g total fat (4 g sat. fat), 65 mg chol., 625 mg sodium, 29 g carbo., 7 g fiber, 26 g pro.

White Bean Chili

START TO FINISH: 50 minutes MAKES: 8 servings

- 1 tablespoon butter
- 1½ cups finely chopped celery
- 1 cup finely chopped onion
- 1 cup finely chopped green sweet pepper
- 3 cloves garlic, minced
- 2 15- to 16-ounce cans Great Northern beans, rinsed and drained
- 2 14-ounce cans chicken broth
- 3 cups cubed cooked chicken or turkey (about 1 pound)
- 1 cup purchased salsa
- 2 teaspoons ground cumin
- 2 bay leaves
- ½ cup half-and-half, light cream, or whipping cream
- 2 tablespoons cornstarch
   Salt and ground black pepper
   Purchased salsa (optional)
   Sliced green onions (optional)

1. In a 4-quart Dutch oven melt butter over medium heat. Add celery, onion, sweet pepper, and garlic; cook until tender. Add beans, chicken broth, chicken, the 1 cup salsa, the cumin, and bay leaves. Bring to boiling; reduce heat. Simmer, uncovered, for 10 minutes.

2. In a screw-top jar combine half-and-half and cornstarch. Cover and shake well; stir into chili. Cook and stir until slightly thickened and bubbly. Cook and stir for 2 minutes more. Season to taste with salt and black pepper. Discard bay leaves.

3. If desired, top individual servings with additional salsa and sliced green onions.

Per serving: 298 cal., 8 g total fat (3 g sat. fat), 57 mg chol., 746 mg sodium, 32 g carbo., 7 g fiber, 25 g pro.

6 Suppertime Salads and Sandwiches

There's nothing light and delicate about these salads and sandwiches! Not only are they quick and easy, they're hearty enough for even the biggest appetites.

Beef and Red Onion Sandwiches

START TO FINISH: 20 minutes **MAKES:** 4 servings

- 8 sliced dried tomatoes or dried tomato halves (not oil packed)
- 2 tablespoons olive oil
- 12 ounces beef sirloin steak, about ³/₄-inch thick
- 1 small red onion, thinly sliced
  Salt and ground black pepper
- 4 square bagels or ciabatta rolls, split
- ¼ cup mayonnaise
- 1 cup mixed salad greens

1. Preheat broiler. Place tomatoes in a small bowl; cover with water. Microwave on 100 percent power (high setting) for 1 minute. Meanwhile, brush oil on steaks and onions; arrange on the unheated rack of a broiler pan. Broil 3 to 4 inches from heat for 12 to 16 minutes or until desired doneness, turning once. Thinly slice beef across the grain into bite-size pieces.

2. Meanwhile, drain tomatoes. Spread split sides of rolls lightly with mayonnaise. Top roll bottoms with steak, onion, drained tomatoes, greens, and roll top.

Per serving: 451 cal., 22 g total fat (4 g sat. fat), 51 mg chol., 681 mg sodium, 40 g carbo., 3 g fiber, 26 g pro.

Garlic-Mustard Steak Sandwiches

PREP: 15 minutes BROIL: 12 minutes MAKES: 4 to 6 servings

    4 to 6 hoagie rolls, split
    2 tablespoons honey mustard
 $1/2$ teaspoon dried marjoram or thyme, crushed
    1 clove garlic, minced
 $1/4$ teaspoon coarsely ground black pepper
    1 1- to $1^1/2$-pound beef flank steak
    1 large red onion, sliced $1/2$ inch thick
    4 to 6 slices Swiss cheese
       Honey mustard (optional)

1. Preheat broiler. Place rolls, cut sides up, on the unheated rack of a broiler pan. Broil 4 to 5 inches from heat for 1 to 2 minutes or until toasted. Set aside. In a bowl, stir together the 2 tablespoons mustard, marjoram, garlic, and pepper.

2. Trim any separable fat from the steak. Score steak on both sides by making shallow diagonal cuts at 1-inch intervals in a diamond pattern. Brush both sides of steak with mustard mixture.

3. Place steak on broiler pan. Place onion slices beside steak. Broil 4 to 5 inches from heat for 12 to 17 minutes or until steak is desired doneness and onion is tender, turning steak and onion slices once.

4. Thinly slice steak at an angle across the grain. Separate onion slices into rings. Arrange steak strips, onion rings, and cheese on roll bottoms. Broil about 1 minute or until cheese starts to melt. Add roll tops. If desired, pass additional mustard.

Per serving: 685 cal., 22 g total fat (9 g sat. fat), 65 mg chol., 844 mg sodium, 78 g carbo., 4 g fiber, 43 g pro.

147

Italian Steak and Cheese Sandwich

START TO FINISH: 25 minutes **MAKES:** 6 serving

- ½ cup mayonnaise
- 2 medium green sweet peppers, cut into rings
- 1 medium onion, sliced
- ¼ cup zesty-style clear Italian salad dressing
- ¾ pound thinly sliced lean roast beef
- 6 French-style rolls, split and toasted
- ½ cup shredded mozzarella cheese (2 ounces)

1. In a large skillet, heat 2 tablespoons of the mayonnaise over medium heat. Add green peppers and onion; cook and stir about 5 minutes or until vegetables are crisp-tender. Remove vegetable mixture from skillet; keep warm.

2. Add remaining mayonnaise and the Italian dressing to skillet. Add meat to skillet; cook over medium heat about 5 minutes or until heated through. Fill rolls with meat mixture and vegetable mixture. Top with cheese.

Per serving: 444 cal., 24 g total fat (5 g sat. fat), 36 mg chol., 956 mg sodium, 37 g carbo., 2 g fiber, 19 g pro.

Ham and Zucchini Wraps and Cranberry Spread

START TO FINISH: 20 minutes MAKES: 4 servings

- ½ of an 8-ounce package cream cheese, softened
- 3 tablespoons dairy sour cream
- ¼ cup finely chopped cranberries
- 2 tablespoons thinly sliced green onion (1)
- 1 teaspoon snipped fresh basil or ¼ teaspoon dried basil, crushed
- 4 8-inch flour tortillas
- 12 ounces thinly sliced deli ham
- 1 small zucchini, cut into bite-size strips (1 cup)
- Fresh basil leaves (optional)

1. For cranberry spread, in a medium mixing bowl beat cream cheese and sour cream with an electric mixer on medium speed until smooth. Stir in cranberries, green onion, and basil.

2. Spread cranberry spread evenly over tortillas. Lay sliced ham over cranberry spread. Lay zucchini strips on ham along one edge. Roll up tortillas tightly. Cut in half crosswise. If desired, garnish with basil leaves.

Per serving: 354 cal., 21 g total fat (10 g sat. fat), 84 mg chol., 1,321 mg sodium, 21 g carbo., 2 g fiber, 29 g pro.

Ham Sandwich with Cranberry Relish

PREP: 20 minutes COOK: 6 minutes MAKES: 6 to 8 servings

  1 tablespoon cooking oil
1½ cups dried cranberries, chopped
  ¾ cup chopped red onion
  ⅓ cup balsamic vinegar
  1 1-pound loaf country-style French bread*
  6 slices Provolone cheese (about 6 ounces)
12 ounces thinly sliced, cooked ham, turkey, and/or turkey-ham
  4 romaine lettuce or red-tip leaf lettuce leaves
  ¼ cup mayonnaise or salad dressing

1. For cranberry relish, in a large skillet heat oil; cook cranberries and onion in the hot oil over medium heat for 5 minutes or until just softened, stirring often. Stir in vinegar; cook and stir about 1 minute more or until most of the liquid is absorbed; let cool.

2. Split loaf of bread in half horizontally. Hollow out inside of each half, leaving a ¾-inch-thick shell. Arrange cheese slices on the bottom half of the bread. Spoon cranberry relish over cheese. Layer meat and lettuce on top of relish. Spread mayonnaise on the cut side of the top half of bread; place spread side down on filled loaf. Cut sandwich into slices.

*TIP: If you buy a round bread loaf, cut the sandwich into wedges.

Per serving: 612 cal., 25 g total fat (8 g sat. fat), 56 mg chol., 1,614 mg sodium, 70 g carbo., 4 g fiber, 27 g pro.

Stuffed Focaccia

START TO FINISH: 20 minutes MAKES: 3 servings

  ½ of a 9- to 10-inch garlic, onion, or plain Italian flat bread (focaccia), split horizontally
  ½ of an 8-ounce container mascarpone cheese
  1 6-ounce jar marinated artichoke hearts, drained and chopped
  1 tablespoon capers, drained
  4 ounces thinly sliced Genoa salami
  1 cup arugula leaves

1. Spread cut sides of focaccia with mascarpone cheese. Sprinkle bottom half of focaccia with artichoke hearts and capers; top with salami and arugula leaves. Add the top of the focaccia, cheese side down. Cut sandwich into thirds.

Per sandwich: 545 cal., 36 g total fat (16 g sat. fat), 83 mg chol., 970 mg sodium, 43 g carbo., 3 g fiber, 23 g pro.

Muffuletta

START TO FINISH: 25 minutes **MAKES:** 6 servings

- I 16-ounce jar pickled mixed vegetables (1½ cups)
- ¼ cup chopped pimiento-stuffed green olives and/or pitted ripe olives
- I clove garlic, minced
- I tablespoon olive oil
- I 16-ounce loaf unsliced French bread
- 6 lettuce leaves
- 6 ounces thinly sliced salami, pepperoni, summer sausage, cooked ham, prosciutto, or a combination
- 6 ounces thinly sliced provolone, Swiss, or mozzarella cheese
- I to 2 medium tomatoes, thinly sliced
- ⅛ teaspoon coarsely ground pepper

I. Drain vegetables, reserving 2 tablespoons liquid. Chop vegetables. Combine vegetables, reserved liquid, olives, garlic, and oil.

2. Split loaf of bread in half horizontally. Hollow out inside of the top half, leaving a 3/4-inch-thick shell.

3. Top the bottom bread half with lettuce leaves, desired meats, desired cheese, and tomato slices. Sprinkle tomato slices with pepper. Stir vegetable mixture. Mound on top of tomato slices. Top with hollowed-out bread half. To serve, slice into 6 portions.

Per serving: 425 cal., 22 g total fat (9 g sat. fat), 42 mg chol., 1,823 mg sodium, 36 g carbo., 2 g fiber, 19 g pro.

Classy Cuban Sandwiches

START TO FINISH: 25 minutes **MAKES:** 4 servings

- 8 ounces thin asparagus spears, trimmed
- 4 hoagie buns or torpedo rolls, split
- 2 to 3 tablespoons coarse-grain mustard
- 8 ounces sliced Swiss cheese
- 6 ounces thinly sliced Serrano ham or any cooked ham
- 6 ounces thinly sliced cooked turkey breast
- Dill pickle slices
- 1 tablespoon olive oil

1. Place asparagus in a microwave-safe 9-inch pie plate or shallow baking dish with 2 tablespoons water; cover with vented plastic wrap. Microwave on 100 percent power (high) for 3 minutes; drain and set aside.

2. Spread bottom halves of rolls with mustard. Top with cheese, asparagus, ham, turkey, and pickle slices. Add roll tops. In a very large skillet or grill pan heat oil over medium heat. Place sandwiches in skillet or grill pan (may need to cook in batches); cover sandwiches in skillet or grill pan with a large heavy heatproof plate and press gently. Cook for 2 to 3 minutes per side or until bread is toasted and cheese is melted.

Per serving: 799 cal., 35 g total fat (15 g sat. fat), 109 mg chol., 2,224 mg sodium, 79 g carbo., 5 g fiber, 42 g pro.

Parmesan Chicken Salad

PREP: 15 minutes **CHILL:** 1 hour **MAKES:** 4 servings

- ½ cup mayonnaise
- 1 tablespoon lemon juice
- 2 teaspoons snipped fresh basil
- 2½ cups chopped cooked chicken or turkey
- ¼ cup grated Parmesan cheese
- ¼ cup thinly sliced green onions
- 3 tablespoons finely chopped celery
- Salt and ground black pepper
- Desired sliced bread

1. For dressing, in a small bowl stir together mayonnaise, lemon juice and basil. Set aside.

2. In a medium bowl combine chicken, Parmesan cheese, green onions and celery. Pour dressing over chicken mixture; toss to coat. Season to taste with salt and ground black pepper. Cover; chill in the refrigerator for 1 to 4 hours.

3. Serve as filling for sandwich.

Per serving: 390 cal., 30 g total fat (6 g sat. fat), 93 mg chol., 604 mg sodium, 2 g carbo., 0 g fiber, 28 g pro.

Cobb Salad Hoagies

START TO FINISH: 35 minutes **MAKES:** 4 servings

- 3 tablespoons olive oil
- 1 tablespoon white wine vinegar
- 1 teaspoon Dijon-style mustard
- 1/2 teaspoon salt
- 1/2 teaspoon ground black pepper
- 1 avocado, halved, seeded, peeled, and finely chopped
- 1 1/3 cups cubed cooked chicken
- 2 roma tomatoes, chopped
- 4 slices bacon, crisp-cooked, drained, and crumbled
- 1/2 cup crumbled blue cheese
- 4 Boston lettuce leaves
- 4 hoagie buns, split, hollowed out, and toasted
- 2 hard-cooked eggs, chopped

1. For dressing, in a small bowl whisk together the olive oil, vinegar, mustard, salt, and pepper. Stir in avocado; set aside.

2. In a medium bowl combine the chicken, tomatoes, bacon, and blue cheese. Pour dressing mixture over chicken mixture and toss to coat. Place lettuce leaves on the bottom halves of the hollowed-out hoagie buns. Spoon chicken mixture on top. Sprinkle with chopped eggs. Top with bun halves.

Per sandwich: 659 cal., 35 g total fat (9 g sat. fat), 165 mg chol., 1,214 mg sodium, 55 g carbo., 5 g fiber, 32 g pro.

Chicken Waldorf Salad Croissants

PREP: 30 minutes COOK: 15 minutes CHILL: 1 hour
MAKES: 6 servings

  5 medium skinless, boneless chicken breast halves (about 1¹/₂ pounds)
  2 cups water
  2 teaspoons instant chicken bouillon granules
  2 apples, chopped
³/₄ cup water
  2 tablespoons lemon juice
  1 cup finely chopped celery
¹/₂ cup mayonnaise, light mayonnaise dressing, or salad dressing
¹/₃ cup broken walnuts, toasted
¹/₃ cup golden raisins
  6 croissants*
     Celery leaves (optional)

1. In a large skillet combine chicken, the 2 cups water, and the chicken bouillon granules. Bring to boiling; reduce heat. Cover and simmer about 15 minutes or until chicken is cooked through. Drain and cool.

2. Toss apples with the ³/₄ cup fresh water and the lemon juice; drain. Chop cooled chicken. In a large bowl, combine chopped chicken, apple, celery, mayonnaise, walnuts, and golden raisins. Cover and chill in the refrigerator for at least 1 hour or up to 4 hours.

3. Serve chicken salad on hollowed-out croissants. If desired, garnish with celery leaves.

*TIP: To serve these sandwiches as appetizers, substitute the 6 full-size croissants with 36 mini croissants. Fill and serve as directed above.

Per serving: 590 cal., 33 g total fat (10 g sat. fat), 111 mg chol., 616 mg sodium, 41 g carbo., 4 g fiber, 33 g pro.

Hot Turkey Sub Sandwiches

PREP: 15 minutes BAKE: 10 minutes MAKES: 4 servings

  1 tablespoon olive oil
  1 teaspoon dried basil, crushed
  $\frac{1}{2}$ teaspoon bottled minced garlic or $\frac{1}{8}$ teaspoon garlic powder
  1 8-ounce loaf or $\frac{1}{2}$ of a 16-ounce loaf unsliced French bread
  6 ounces sliced mozzarella cheese
  4 ounces sliced smoked turkey
  2 tablespoons sliced pitted ripe olives
  2 tomatoes, thinly sliced
  $\frac{1}{8}$ teaspoon coarsely ground black pepper

1. Preheat oven to 375°F. In a small bowl stir together olive oil, basil, and garlic. Cut French bread in half horizontally. Using a spoon, hollow out the top half of bread, leaving a $\frac{3}{4}$-inch shell. Brush cut sides of both halves with olive oil mixture.

2. On the bottom half of bread layer half of the mozzarella cheese, all of the smoked turkey, the olives, the remaining cheese, and the tomato slices. Sprinkle with pepper. Replace the top half of bread. Wrap sandwich in heavy foil.

3. Bake about 10 minutes or until heated through.

Per serving: 335 cal., 13 g total fat (5 g sat. fat), 36 mg chol., 849 mg sodium, 33 g carbo., 1 g fiber, 22 g pro.

Fish Sandwich with Basil Mayonnaise

PREP: 20 minutes BAKE: 4 minutes MAKES: 4 servings

- 3 tablespoons mayonnaise or salad dressing
- 2 tablespoons dairy sour cream
- 2 tablespoons snipped fresh basil or 1/2 teaspoon dried basil, crushed
- 1/2 teaspoon finely shredded lemon peel
- 1 pound fresh or frozen skinless fish fillets, about 1/2 inch thick
- 1/4 cup milk
- 1/2 cup fine dry bread crumbs
- 1/4 teaspoon paprika
- 1/8 teaspoon salt
- 1/8 teaspoon ground black pepper
- 2 tablespoons butter, melted
- 4 hamburger buns or kaiser rolls, split and toasted
  Lettuce leaves

1. In a small bowl stir together mayonnaise, sour cream, basil, and lemon peel. Cover and chill until serving time. Thaw fish, if frozen.

2. Preheat oven to 500°F. Rinse fish; pat dry with paper towels. Cut fish into 4 serving-size portions; set aside. Grease a shallow baking pan; set aside.

3. Pour milk into a shallow dish. In another shallow dish combine bread crumbs, paprika, salt, and pepper. Dip fish in milk and roll in crumb mixture to coat. Place fish in the prepared baking pan, tucking under any thin edges. Drizzle with melted butter.

4. Bake, uncovered, for 4 to 6 minutes or until fish flakes easily when tested when tested with a fork and coating is golden brown. Serve fish in buns with lettuce and Basil Mayonnaise.

Per serving: 399 cal., 22 g total fat (5 g sat. fat), 30 mg chol., 529 mg sodium, 29 g carbo., I g fiber, 21 g pro.

Open-Face Ratatouille Sandwich

PREP: 25 minutes ROAST: 45 minutes MAKES: 4 servings

Nonstick cooking spray

1 small eggplant, cut in 1-inch pieces

1 small zucchini or yellow summer squash, cut into ¾-inch slices

1 medium red sweet pepper, cut in strips

½ of a small red onion, cut in ½-inch wedges

1 tablespoon olive oil

½ teaspoon herbes de Provence or dried thyme, crushed

2 medium plum tomatoes, each cut lengthwise in 6 wedges

8 small or 4 large ½-inch slices whole wheat or white French bread, toasted (about 8 ounces total)

1 clove garlic, halved

2 tablespoons balsamic vinegar

Fresh thyme sprigs (optional)

1. Preheat oven to 400°F. Coat a large shallow roasting pan with cooking spray. Add eggplant, zucchini, sweet pepper, and onion to prepared pan. Drizzle with olive oil; sprinkle with herbes de Provence, ⅛ teaspoon *salt*, and ⅛ teaspoon *black pepper*. Toss to coat. Roast vegetables 30 minutes, tossing once. Add tomatoes to roasting pan. Roast 15 to 20 minutes more or until vegetables are tender and some surface areas are lightly browned.

2. Meanwhile, rub toasted bread with cut sides of the garlic clove. Place two small slices or one large slice of the bread on each of four serving plates. Sprinkle balsamic vinegar over vegetables; toss gently to coat. Spoon warm vegetables on bread. If desired, garnish with fresh thyme sprigs.

Per serving: 250 cal., 7 g total fat (1 g sat. fat), 0 mg chol., 328 mg sodium, 43 g carbo., 8 g fiber, 7 g pro.

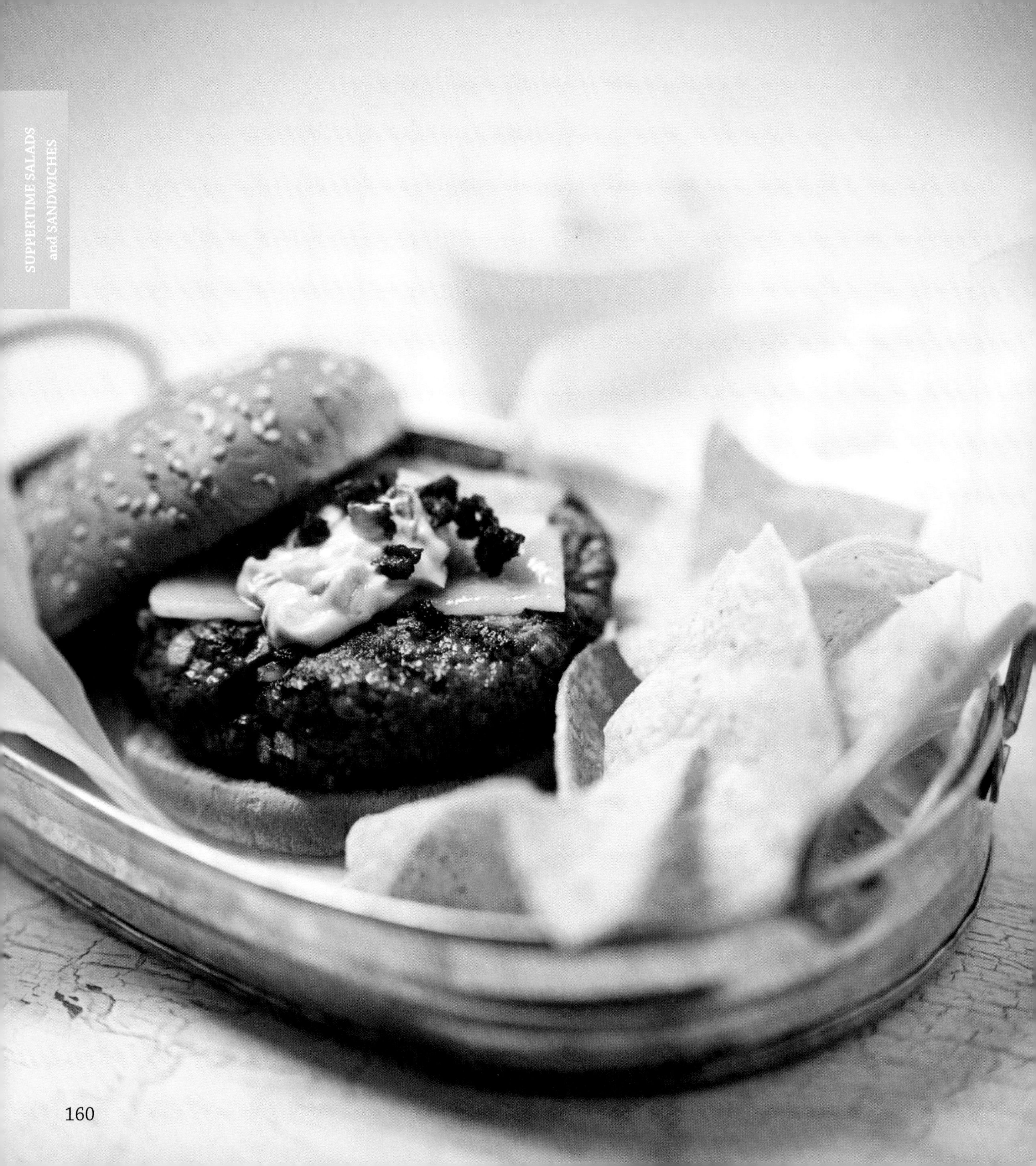

Two-Pepper Burgers

PREP: 20 minutes **GRILL:** 14 minutes **MAKES:** 6 servings

- ¹/₂ cup mayonnaise or salad dressing
- ¹/₂ to I canned chipotle pepper in adobo sauce, finely chopped
- 3 to 5 fresh jalapeño chile peppers (see note, page 75)
- ¹/₃ cup finely chopped onion
- 4 cloves garlic, minced
- 2 teaspoons Cajun or Creole seasoning
- I¹/₂ pounds ground beef
- 4 ounces Monterey Jack cheese, sliced
- 6 hamburger buns, split and toasted

I. In a small bowl combine mayonnaise and chipotle pepper. Cover and chill until serving time. Seed and finely chop the jalapeño peppers. In a large bowl combine jalapeños, onion, garlic, and Cajun seasoning. Add ground beef; mix well. Shape mixture into six ³/₄-inch-thick patties.

2. For charcoal grill, place patties on the rack of an uncovered grill directly over medium coals. Grill for 14 to 18 minutes or until an instant-read thermometer inserted in center of patties registers 160°F, turning once halfway through grilling. (For gas grill, preheat grill. Reduce heat to medium. Place patties on grill rack directly over medium heat; cover and grill as above.) Top with cheese slices; grill about 30 seconds more or until cheese is melted. Serve on buns with mayonnaise-pepper mixture.

TIP: To broil burgers, place burgers on the unheated rack of a broiler pan. Broil 3 to 4 inches from heat for 12 to 14 minutes or until instant-read thermometer inserted in center of patties registers 160°F, turning once halfway through broiling.

Per serving: 557 cal., 38 g total fat (12 g sat. fat), 93 mg chol., 578 mg sodium, 24 g carbo., 2 g fiber, 29 g pro.

Fire and Spice Beef Burgers

PREP: 25 minutes **BROIL:** 11 minutes **MAKES:** 44 servings

- I egg, slightly beaten
- ³/₄ cup soft bread crumbs
- ¹/₃ cup finely chopped onion
- 2 tablespoons plain yogurt
- ¹/₂ teaspoon salt
- ¹/₂ teaspoon ground cinnamon or ground cardamom
- ¹/₂ teaspoon ground coriander or mace
- ¹/₄ teaspoon cayenne pepper
- I pound ground beef, lamb or pork
- ¹/₄ cup jalapeño or hot pepper jelly
- 4 lettuce leaves
- 2 large pita bread rounds, halved crosswise
  - Thinly sliced cucumber (optional)
  - Plain yogurt (optional)

I. Preheat broiler. In a large bowl combine egg and bread crumbs. Stir in onion, the 2 tablespoons yogurt, salt, cinnamon, coriander and cayenne pepper. Add ground meat; mix well. Shape mixture into 4 oval patties, each about 5 inches long and ¹/₂ inch thick.

2. Place patties on the unheated rack of a broiler pan. Broil 3 to 4 inches from the heat for 11 to 13 minutes or until done (160°F), turning meat halfway through broiling, brushing once with 2 tablespoons of the jalapeño jelly. Spoon remaining jelly over patties before serving. Serve burgers in lettuce-lined pita halves with cucumber slices and additional yogurt, if desired.

Per serving: 410 cal., 16 g total fat (6 g sat. fat), 125 mg chol., 585 mg sodium, 37 g carbo., 2 g fiber, 28 g pro.

Italian-American Cheeseburgers

RISE: 15 minutes GRILL: 14 minutes MAKES: 6 servings

1½ pounds lean ground beef
1 cup crumbled Gorgonzola cheese (4 ounces)
⅓ cup snipped dried oil-pack tomatoes
1 tablespoon snipped fresh thyme
4 cloves garlic, minced
½ teaspoon salt
½ teaspoon coarsely ground black pepper
6 sourdough rolls, split and toasted
    Sliced red onions
    Sliced tomatoes

1. In a large mixing bowl combine beef, ³/₄ cup of the Gorgonzola cheese, all but 1 tablespoon of the snipped dried tomatoes, the thyme, garlic, salt, and pepper; mix well. Shape mixture into six ³/₄-inch thick patties.

2. For a charcoal grill, place burger patties on the lightly oiled rack of an uncovered grill directly over medium heat. Grill for 14 to 18 minutes or until an instant-read thermometer inserted in centers registers 160°F, turning burgers once halfway through grilling. (For a gas grill, preheat grill. Reduce heat to medium. Place burger patties on grill rack directly over heat. Cover and grill as above.)

3. Remove burgers from grill. Top with remaining Gorgonzola and snipped dried tomatoes. Serve on toasted sourdough rolls with sliced red onions and tomatoes.

TIP: To broil burgers, place burgers on unheated rack of broiler pan. Broil 3 to 4 inches from the heat for 12 to 14 minutes or until an instant-read thermometer inserted in centers registers 160°F, turning burgers once halfway through broiling.

Per serving: 385 cal., 17 g total fat (8 g sat. fat), 85 mg chol., 723 mg sodium, 27 g carbo., 0 g fiber, 29 g pro.

Hot and Spicy Sloppy Joe

PREP: 30 minutes COOK: 50 minutes MAKES: 14 to 16 servings

2	pounds ground beef
4	medium green sweet peppers, chopped (3 cups)
2	medium red sweet peppers, chopped (1½ cups)
4	medium onions, chopped (2 cups)
2	cups strong coffee
1	cup cider vinegar
1½	cups ketchup
2	teaspoons chili powder
2	teaspoons paprika
½	teaspoon salt
½	teaspoon ground black pepper
1	Scotch bonnet chile pepper, seeded and finely chopped (see note, page 75), or ¼ teaspoon cayenne pepper
14	to 16 hamburger or hot dog buns, split and toasted if desired

1. In a 4-quart Dutch oven cook ground beef, green and red sweet peppers, and onions until meat is brown and vegetables are tender. Drain off fat.

2. Stir in coffee and vinegar. Bring to boiling. Boil gently, uncovered, over medium heat for about 40 minutes or until most of the liquid is evaporated, stirring occasionally.

3. Stir in ketchup, chili powder, paprika, salt, black pepper, and Scotch bonnet or cayenne. Cook and stir 10 to 15 minutes more or until desired consistency. Serve meat in buns.

Per serving: 283 cal., 9 g total fat (3 g sat. fat), 41 mg chol., 658 mg sodium, 36 g carbo., 3 g fiber, 17 g pro.

Dazzling Sirloin Salad

PREP: 20 minutes COOK: 17 minutes BROIL: 12 minutes
MAKES: 4 servings

- 1 tablespoon butter
- 1 cup finely chopped onion
- 2 tablespoons sugar
- 1/3 cup extra-virgin olive oil
- 1/4 cup balsamic vinegar
- 2 tablespoons red wine vinegar
- 1 tablespoon lemon juice
- 1 teaspoon soy sauce
- 1 head romaine lettuce (1 pound), torn
- 4 plum tomatoes, cored and quartered
- 1/2 cup crumbled blue cheese (2 ounces)
- 6 radishes, thinly sliced
- 1 tablespoon snipped fresh parsley
- 1 tablespoon capers, drained
- 3/4 pound boneless beef sirloin steak, cut 1-inch thick

1. In a medium skillet melt butter over medium heat. Add onion. Reduce heat to medium-low and cook for 15 to 20 minutes or until the onion is very soft and golden, stirring occasionally. Sprinkle sugar over the onion and cook, stirring frequently, for 7 to 10 minutes more or until the onion starts to brown. Remove from the heat. Cool the cooked onion slightly.

2. In a screw-top jar combine the caramelized onion with olive oil, balsamic vinegar, red wine vinegar, lemon juice, and soy sauce. Cover mixture and shake well. Season to taste with salt and pepper.

3. Divide the romaine among 4 individual dinner plates. Arrange 1/4 of the tomatoes, blue cheese, radishes, parsley, and the capers on each serving plate of greens. Set aside.

4. Slash fat edges of steak at 1-inch intervals, being careful not to cut into the meat. Place the steak on the unheated rack of a broiler pan. Broil the meat 3 to 4 inches from the heat for 6 minutes. Turn the steak. Broil the meat to desired doneness. Allow 6 to 8 minutes more for medium (155°F) or 8 to 10 minutes more for well done (165°F).

5. Remove meat from the pan. Cover cooked steak with foil and let stand for 5 minutes before cutting into bite-size strips. (The internal temperature of the meat will rise 5°F during standing time.) Arrange steak strips on top of the salad. Drizzle about 2 tablespoons of the caramelized onion dressing over each salad.

Per serving: 440 cal., 30 g total fat 70 mg chol., 508 mg sodium, 21 g carbo., 4 g fiber, 24 g pro.

Steak Salad with Buttermilk Dressing

START TO FINISH: 30 minutes MAKES: 4 servings

- 8 cups torn, mixed salad greens
- 2 medium carrots, cut into thin bite-size strips
- 1 medium yellow sweet pepper, cut into thin bite-size strips
- 1 cup cherry or pear-shaped tomatoes, halved
- 8 ounces boneless beef top sirloin steak
  Nonstick cooking spray
- 1/4 cup finely shredded fresh basil
  Salt and ground black pepper
- 1/2 to 3/4 cup bottled ranch salad dressing or Parmesan ranch salad dressing

1. Arrange salad greens, carrots, sweet pepper, and tomatoes on 4 dinner plates. Set aside. Trim fat from meat. Cut meat across the grain into thin bite-size strips.

2. Lightly coat a large skillet with cooking spray. Heat over medium-high heat. Add meat. Cook and stir for 2 to 3 minutes or until meat is slightly pink in the center. Remove from heat. Stir in basil. Lightly sprinkle with additional salt and black pepper to taste.

3. To serve, spoon the warm meat mixture over greens mixture. Drizzle with buttermilk dressing. Serve immediately.

Per serving: 263 cal., 17 g total fat (3 g sat. fat), 33 mg chol., 366 mg sodium, 13 g carbo., 4 g fiber, 15 g pro.

Steak Salad with Cilantro Oil

PREP: 25 minutes MARINATE: 2 hours GRILL: 12 minutes
MAKES: 4 servings

12 ounces beef flank steak or boneless sirloin steak, cut 1-inch thick
1/8 teaspoon salt
1/8 teaspoon ground black pepper
1/3 cup packed fresh cilantro
2 tablespoons olive oil
1/2 clove garlic, minced
1/8 teaspoon bottled hot pepper sauce
1/4 cup lime juice
6 cups small romaine lettuce leaves
5 ounces jicama, peeled and cut into 2-inch sticks (1 cup)
1 medium mango, sliced
1 small red onion, cut in thin wedges
2 teaspoons honey

1. Season steak with salt and pepper. Place in a self-sealing plastic bag set in a shallow bowl. Set aside.

2. In a small bowl combine cilantro, olive oil, garlic, and hot pepper sauce. Add lime juice. Pour half the juice mixture over meat. Seal bag. Marinate in refrigerator for 2 to 24 hours. Cover and chill remaining lime-cilantro mixture for dressing.

3. Drain meat. Discard marinade. For a charcoal grill, place meat on rack of an uncovered grill directly over medium coals. Grill for 12 to 14 minutes for medium doneness, turning once. (For a gas grill, preheat grill. Reduce heat to medium. Place meat on grill rack directly over heat. Cover and grill as above.) Remove from grill. Thinly slice across grain.

4. To serve, divide romaine leaves among 4 individual salad bowls. Top with steak slices, jicama, mango, and onion. In a bowl combine reserved lime-cilantro mixture and honey. Drizzle over salad.

TIP: To broil meat, place meat on the unheated rack of a broiler pan. Broil 3 to 4 inches from the heat to desired doneness. (Allow 15 to 18 minutes for flank steak and 15 to 20 minutes for sirloin.)

Per serving: 274 cal., 13 g total fat (3 g sat. fat), 34 mg chol., 131 mg sodium, 20 g carbo., 3 g fiber, 21 g pro.

Blackberry Salad with Pork

PREP: 25 minutes ROAST: 25 minutes MAKES: 4 servings

    1 12- to 16-ounce pork tenderloin
       Salt and ground black pepper
    ¼ cup olive oil
    ¼ cup honey
    ¼ cup lemon juice
    6 cups packaged mixed baby greens (spring mix)
    2 cups blackberries, raspberries, and/or sliced strawberries
    1 cup grape tomatoes (halved, if desired)
    ½ cup pine nuts, toasted*
    4 ounces Brie cheese, rind removed, if desired, and cut into wedges

1. Preheat oven to 425° F. Place pork on a rack in a shallow roasting pan. Sprinkle with salt and pepper. Roast, uncovered, for 25 to 35 minutes or until an instant-read thermometer inserted in center registers 155° F. Remove from oven. Cover with foil and let stand until temperature registers 160° F. Cool slightly. Slice pork ¼ inch thick.

2. For dressing, in a screw-top jar combine oil, honey, lemon juice, and salt and pepper to taste; cover and shake well.

3. To serve, in salad bowls or on individual plates, place greens; top with berries, tomatoes, pine nuts, Brie wedges, and pork slices. Drizzle with dressing. Serve immediately.

*TIP: To toast nuts, place nuts in a shallow baking pan. Bake in a 350° F oven for 5 to 7 minutes, shaking pan once or twice. Watch closely so nuts don't burn.

Per serving: 569 cal., 36 g total fat (10 g sat. fat), 95 mg chol., 308 mg sodium, 32 g carbo., 5 g fiber, 37 g pro.

Smoked Pork Salad

PREP: 15 minutes COOK: 8 minutes MARINATE: 2 hours
MAKES: 4 servings

- 4 boneless cooked smoked pork chops, cut ¾-inch thick
- 1 tablespoon cooking oil
- 6 cups torn Boston or Bibb lettuce
- 8 pear or grape tomatoes, halved
- 2 ounces Gouda or white cheddar cheese, cut into bite-size pieces
- ½ cup bottled low-carb oil-and-vinegar salad dressing
- 2 teaspoons Dijon-style mustard
- 1 teaspoon snipped fresh thyme

1. In a large skillet cook meat in hot oil for 8 to 10 minutes or until hot, turning once.

2. Meanwhile, divide lettuce, tomatoes, and cheese among 4 salad plates. In a small bowl whisk together salad dressing, mustard, and thyme. Drizzle some of the dressing over salads. Thinly slice meat; arrange slices on top of salads. Serve with remaining dressing.

Per serving: 386 cal., 29 g total fat (8 g sat. fat), 77 mg chol., 1,629 mg sodium, 5 g carbo., 1 g fiber, 26 g pro.

Ham and Chutney Pasta Salad

START TO FINISH: 25 minutes Makes: 4 servings

    8 ounces packaged dried medium shell macaroni
 $^1/_2$ cup chutney
 $^1/_2$ cup mayonnaise or salad dressing
    2 green onions, sliced ($^1/_4$ cup)
 $^1/_8$ teaspoon coarsely ground black pepper
 $1^1/_2$ cups cubed cooked ham (8 ounces)
    4 lettuce leaves
       Cherry tomato wedges (optional)

I. Cook macaroni according to package directions. Drain. Rinse with cold water. Drain again.

2. Meanwhile, cut up any large pieces of chutney. Stir together the chutney, mayonnaise, green onions, and pepper.

3. Toss together the chilled macaroni, chutney mixture, and ham. Line 4 salad plates with lettuce leaves. Serve ham mixture on lettuce-lined plates. If desired, garnish with cherry tomatoes.

Per serving: 580 cal., 26 g total fat (4 g sat. fat), 46 mg chol., 850 mg sodium, 66 g carbo., 2 g fiber, 20 g pro.

Spring Greens and Roasted Chicken

START TO FINISH: 25 minutes MAKES: 6 servings

- 1 2¼-pound purchased roasted chicken, chilled
- 1 5-ounce package mixed spring greens salad mix (about 8 cups)
- 2 cups fresh sliced strawberries or blueberries
- 4 ounces Gorgonzola or blue cheese, crumbled (1 cup)
- ½ cup honey roasted cashews or peanuts
- 1 lemon, halved
- 3 tablespoons olive oil
- ¼ teaspoon salt
- ¼ teaspoon ground black pepper
- ½ cup honey-roasted cashews or peanuts

1. Remove string from chicken, if present. Remove and discard skin from chicken. Pull meat from bones, discarding bones. Shred meat (you should have about 3½ cups).

2. Place greens on a platter. Top with chicken, berries, cheese and nuts. Drizzle with juice from lemon and oil; sprinkle with salt and pepper. Sprinkle with nuts.

Per serving: 426 cal., 31 g total fat (9 g sat. fat), 81 mg chol., 482 mg sodium, 12 g carbo., 2 g fiber, 28 g pro.

Strawberry Chicken Salad with Warm Citrus Dressing

PREP: 30 minutes MAKES: 4 servings

- 4 medium skinless, boneless chicken breast halves (about 1 pound)
- 1 14-ounce can chicken broth
- 2½ cups strawberries
- ⅓ cup orange juice
- 2 tablespoons salad oil
- 2 teaspoons finely shredded lemon peel
- 1 tablespoon lemon juice
- 1 teaspoon sugar
- ½ teaspoon chili powder
- ¼ teaspoon salt
- ¼ teaspoon freshly ground black pepper
- 6 cups torn spinach, watercress, and/or other greens
- ¼ cup chopped walnuts, toasted

1. Sprinkle the chicken breast halves lightly with salt and pepper. Pour chicken broth into a large saucepan or skillet; add chicken to broth. Bring broth to boiling; reduce heat. Cover and simmer chicken for 15 to 20 minutes or until chicken is tender and no longer pink. Remove chicken from broth with a slotted spoon and cool slightly. (Save broth and use later for chicken soup.)

2. Meanwhile, in a blender or food processor combine ½ cup of the strawberries, orange juice, salad oil, lemon peel, lemon juice, sugar, chili powder, salt, and black pepper. Cover; blend or process until smooth. Transfer to a small saucepan. Bring just to boiling. Simmer, uncovered, 5 minutes, stirring occasionally. Keep warm until needed.

3. Thinly slice chicken breasts. In a large bowl, toss together the salad greens, remaining strawberries, and chicken.

4. To serve, drizzle warm dressing over salad. Sprinkle with nuts. Serve immediately.

MAKE-AHEAD DIRECTIONS: Prepare the salad but not the dressing. Cover salad and chill up to 4 hours. Prepare dressing and serve as above.

Per serving: 287 cal., 14 g total fat (2 g sat. fat), 66 mg chol., 677 mg sodium, 12 g carbo., 7 g fiber, 31 g pro.

Pommery Chicken Salad

PREP: 25 minutes CHILL: 1 hour MAKES: 4 servings

- 1/4 cup mayonnaise
- 2 tablespoons creamy Dijon-style mustard blend
- 2 tablespoons coarse-grain brown mustard
- 2 1/2 cups chopped cooked chicken or turkey
- 1/4 cup finely chopped celery
- 1/4 cup thinly sliced green onions (2)
- 2 tablespoons pine nuts, toasted
- 1 tablespoon snipped fresh parsley
- 1 tablespoon drained and finely chopped oil-packed dried tomatoes
  Salt and ground black pepper
  Croissants or sourdough bread

1. For dressing, in a small bowl, stir together mayonnaise and mustards. Set aside.

2. In a medium bowl, combine chicken, celery, green onions, pine nuts, parsley, and tomatoes. Season to taste with salt and ground black pepper. Pour dressing over chicken mixture; toss to coat. Cover; chill in the refrigerator for 1 to 4 hours.

3. Serve on croissants or sourdough bread.

Per serving: 556 cal., 34 g total fat (10 g sat. fat), 121 mg chol., 882 mg sodium, 29 g carbo., 2 g fiber, 31 g pro.

Turkey Salad Platter

START TO FINISH: 25 minutes MAKES: 6 servings

- 1 pound chopped cooked smoked turkey breast
- 2 stalks celery, sliced 1/2 inch thick
- 1/2 cup mayonnaise or salad dressing
- 1/4 teaspoon cracked black pepper
- 8 cups mixed baby salad greens
- 1 medium orange, cut into wedges
- 1/2 of a small red onion, thinly sliced and separated into rings (1/4 cup)
- 1/2 cup bottled raspberry vinaigrette
- 1/2 cup dried cranberries
- 1/2 cup broken walnuts, toasted

1. In a medium mixing bowl combine turkey, celery, mayonnaise, and pepper. Cover and chill until serving time, if desired.

2. To assemble, spoon turkey mixture onto a large serving platter. Place salad greens and orange wedges around the turkey mixture. Top greens with red onions. Drizzle raspberry vinaigrette over greens. Top turkey mixture and greens with cranberries and toasted walnuts.

Per serving: 400 cal., 30 g total fat (4 g sat. fat), 39 mg chol., 880 mg sodium, 17 g carbo., 3 g fiber, 19 g pro.

Ginger Shrimp Pasta Salad

PREP: 30 minutes CHILL: 2 hours MAKES: 8 servings

1¹/₂ pounds fresh or frozen medium shrimp
1 tablespoon olive oil
2 cloves garlic, minced
1 tablespoon grated fresh ginger
8 ounces dried penne pasta
¹/₄ cup sherry vinegar or white wine vinegar
¹/₄ cup olive oil
1¹/₂ cups halved yellow or red pear tomatoes or grape tomatoes
1 cup chopped red or yellow sweet pepper
1 stalk celery, finely chopped
¹/₄ cup finely chopped red onion
¹/₄ cup snipped fresh basil
1 tablespoon capers, drained
   Salt and ground black pepper

1. Thaw shrimp, if frozen. Peel and devein shrimp, leaving tails intact, if desired. Rinse shrimp; pat dry with paper towels. In a large skillet, heat the 1 tablespoon oil over medium heat. Add garlic and ginger; cook and stir for 15 seconds. Add shrimp; cook about 3 minutes or until shrimp are opaque, stirring frequently. Set aside.

2. Meanwhile, cook pasta according to package directions. Drain. Rinse pasta with cold water; drain again.

3. In a very large bowl whisk together vinegar and the ¹/₄ cup oil. Add cooked pasta and shrimp; toss to coat. Stir in tomatoes, sweet pepper, celery, red onion, basil, and capers. Season to taste with salt and black pepper. Cover and chill for 2 to 24 hours.

Per serving: 267 cal., 10 g total fat (1 g sat. fat), 97 mg chol., 122 mg sodium, 26 g carbo., 2 g fiber, 17 g pro.

Spinach-Pasta Salad with Shrimp

START TO FINISH: 25 minutes MAKES: 6 servings

- 1 cup shell pasta or elbow macaroni
- 1 pound frozen cooked shrimp, thawed or 1 pound cooked deli shrimp
- 1 cup chopped red sweet pepper
- 1/3 cup bottled creamy onion or Caesar salad dressing
- 2 tablespoons snipped fresh dill (optional)
  Salt and freshly ground black pepper
- 1 6-ounce package baby spinach
- 4 ounces goat cheese, sliced or feta cheese, crumbled
  Bottled creamy onion or Caesar dressing (optional)

1. Cook pasta according to package directions; drain.

2. In an extra large bowl combine cooked pasta, shrimp, and sweet pepper. Drizzle with 1/3 cup salad dressing; sprinkle with dill, if desired. Toss to coat. Season to taste with salt and pepper. Divide spinach between salad plates or bowls. Top with shrimp mixture and cheese. Drizzle with additional dressing, if desired.

Per serving: 247 cal., 10 g total fat (4 g sat. fat), 156 mg chol., 435 mg sodium, 17 g carbo., 2 g fiber, 23 g pro.

7 Serve-Along Side Dishes

What's a meal without great side dishes? Here you'll find something to go with every main dish in this book!

Sour Cream and Chive Mashed Potatoes

PREP: 15 minutes   COOK: 20 minutes   MAKES : 8 to 10 servings

- 1   5-pound bag baking potatoes (such as russet or Yukon gold), peeled, if desired, and quartered
- 1   tablespoon salt
- 1   8-ounce carton dairy sour cream
- ⅓   cup butter
- ½   teaspoon salt
- ¼   teaspoon ground black pepper
- ½   to ¾ cup milk
- ¼   cup snipped fresh chives
-     Snipped fresh chives (optional)

1. In a 6-quart Dutch oven cook potatoes and the 1 tablespoon salt, covered, in enough boiling water to cover for 20 to 25 minutes or until tender; drain.

2. Mash with a potato masher or beat with an electric mixer on low speed. Add sour cream, butter, the ½ teaspoon salt, and pepper. Gradually beat in enough of the milk to make mixture light and fluffy. Just before serving, stir in the ¼ cup chives. If desired, sprinkle with additional chives.

Per serving: 355 cal., 14 g total fat (9 g sat. fat), 34 mg chol., 529 mg sodium, 52 g carbo., 6 g fiber, 8 g pro.

GARLIC MASHED POTATOES: Prepare as above, except add 10 peeled garlic cloves to water while cooking potatoes, omit the sour cream and chives, and substitute ⅓ cup olive oil for the butter.

PESTO MASHED POTATOES: Prepare as above, except omit sour cream and chives and add ⅓ cup purchased basil pesto along with the butter.

Shredded Hash Browns

START TO FINISH: 25 minutes MAKES: 2 to 3 servings

- 3 or 4 small russet or white potatoes (about 12 ounces total)
- ¼ cup finely chopped onion
- 1 small fresh jalapeño chile pepper, banana pepper, or Anaheim chile pepper, seeded and chopped* (optional) (see note, page 75)
- ¼ teaspoon salt
- ⅛ teaspoon coarsely ground black pepper
- 2 tablespoons butter, cooking oil, or margarine
    Fresh sage leaves (optional)

1. Peel potatoes and coarsely shred using the coarsest side of the shredder (you should have about 2 cups shredded potatoes). Rinse shredded potatoes in a colander; drain well and pat dry with paper towels. In a medium bowl combine shredded potatoes, onion, chile pepper (if using), salt, and black pepper.

2. In a large nonstick skillet melt butter over medium heat. Carefully add potato mixture, pressing into an even pancake-like round (7 to 8 inches in diameter). Using a spatula, press potato mixture firmly. Cover and cook over medium heat about 8 minutes or until golden brown. Check occasionally and reduce heat, if necessary, to prevent overbrowning.

3. Using two spatulas or a spatula and fork, turn the hash browns. (If you're not sure you can turn in a single flip, cut into quarters and turn by sections.) Cook, uncovered, for 5 to 7 minutes more or until golden brown and crisp. Remove from skillet; cut into wedges. If desired, garnish with fresh sage.

Per serving: 168 cal., 9 g total fat (1 g sat. fat), 0 mg chol., 197 mg sodium, 19 g carbo., 2 g fiber, 3 g pro.

Dilled Broccoli-Potato Salad

PREP: 20 minutes **CHILL:** 6 hours **MAKES:** 8 to 10 servings

- 2 pounds red potatoes
- ⅓ cup chicken broth
- ⅓ cup cider vinegar
- 1 tablespoon snipped fresh dill or 1 teaspoon dried dillweed
- 1 tablespoon cooking oil
- 1 teaspoon sugar
- ½ teaspoon salt
- ½ teaspoon pepper
- ¾ cup chopped red onion
- 3 cups small broccoli florets
- ½ cup finely shredded Parmesan cheese (1 ounce)

1. Scrub the potatoes; cut into ½-inch cubes. In large covered saucepan, cook potato cubes in a small amount of boiling salted water for 8 to 10 minutes or just until tender. Drain; cool.

2. In small bowl whisk together broth, vinegar, dill, oil, sugar, salt and pepper. In a large bowl, combine cooled potatoes and onion. Pour broth mixture over; toss to combine. Cover and refrigerate at least 6 hours or up to 24 hours.

3. Meanwhile in a medium covered saucepan cook broccoli in small amount of boiling water for 2 to 3 minutes or until bright green and just tender. Drain; cover and chill until needed. Just before serving, toss broccoli with the potato mixture. Sprinkle with shredded Parmesan cheese. Season to taste with salt and pepper.

Per serving: 156 cal., 3 g total fat 3 mg chol., 223 mg sodium, 29 g carbo., 2 g fiber, 5 g pro.

180

Ginger-Peanut Pasta Salad

PREP: 25 minutes CHILL: 2 hours MAKES: 12 servings

- 8 ounces corkscrew macaroni or fine noodles, broken up
- 20 fresh pea pods, tips and strings removed (about 1 cup)
- 1 small cucumber, quartered lengthwise and sliced
- 2 medium carrots, cut into long thin strips (about 1 cup)
- 1 medium yellow and/or green sweet pepper, cut into thin strips
- ¾ cup thinly sliced radishes
- ½ cup bias-sliced green onions (4)
- 3 tablespoons snipped fresh cilantro or parsley
   Ginger Salad Dressing (see recipe, right)
- ⅓ cup chopped peanuts

1. Cook pasta according to package directions. During the last 30 seconds of cooking time, add pea pods; drain. Rinse with cold water and drain thoroughly.

2. Combine pasta and pea pod mixture, cucumber, carrots, sweet pepper, radishes, green onions, and cilantro or parsley in a large bowl. Add Ginger Salad Dressing, and toss gently to coat. Cover and chill for 2 to 8 hours.

3. To serve, toss the salad again and sprinkle with peanuts.

GINGER SALAD DRESSING: In a screw-top jar combine ¼ cup salad oil, 3 tablespoons rice vinegar, 2 tablespoons sugar, 2 tablespoons soy sauce, 1 teaspoon grated gingerroot, and 1 teaspoon chili oil or several dashes bottled hot pepper sauce. Cover and shake to combine. Chill up to 3 days. Shake before using.

Per serving: 165 cal., 7 g total fat (1 g sat. fat), 0 mg chol., 197 mg sodium, 21 g carbo., 1 g fiber, 4 g pro.

Orzo-Broccoli Pilaf

PREP: 20 minutes **COOK:** 15 minutes **STAND:** 5 minutes
MAKES: 6 servings

    2 teaspoons olive oil
    1 cup sliced fresh mushrooms
    ½ cup chopped onion
    ⅔ cup dry orzo pasta (rosamarina)
    1 14-ounce can reduced-sodium chicken broth
    ½ cup shredded carrot
    1 teaspoon dried marjoram, crushed
    ⅛ teaspoon ground black pepper
    2 cups small broccoli florets

1. In a large saucepan heat olive oil over medium-high heat. Cook and stir the mushrooms and onion in hot oil until onion is tender. Stir in the orzo. Cook and stir about 2 minutes more or until orzo is lightly browned. Remove from heat.

2. Carefully stir in the chicken broth, carrot, marjoram, and pepper. Bring to boiling; reduce heat. Cover and simmer about 15 minutes or until orzo is tender but still firm. Remove saucepan from heat; stir in broccoli. Let stand, covered, for 5 minutes.

Per serving: 113 cal., 2 g total fat (0 g sat. fat), 0 mg chol., 209 mg sodium, 19 g carbo., 2 g fiber, 4 g pro.

Savory Squash Pilaf

START TO FINISH: 35 minutes MAKES: 4 to 6 servings

- ⅓ cup finely chopped onion
- 1 tablespoon walnut oil or cooking oil
- ⅔ cup uncooked long grain rice
- 3 tablespoons golden raisins
- ¼ teaspoon ground allspice
- 1⅓ cups reduced-sodium chicken broth
- 1½ cups peeled, seeded, and cubed winter squash (such as acorn, butternut, or buttercup)
- 2 teaspoons snipped fresh Italian (flat-leaf) parsley
  Fresh Italian (flat-leaf) parsley sprigs

1. In a medium saucepan cook and stir onion in hot oil over medium heat about 4 minutes or just until tender. Stir in rice, raisins, and allspice. Carefully stir in broth. Bring to boiling; reduce heat. Simmer, covered, for 5 minutes. Stir in squash cubes. Cook for 10 to 12 minutes more or until rice is tender but still firm and squash is just tender. Remove saucepan from heat; stir in snipped parsley. If desired, garnish with parsley sprigs.

Per serving: 189 cal., 4 g total fat (0 g sat. fat), 0 mg chol., 211 mg sodium, 35 g carbo., 1 g fiber, 4 g pro.

Zucchini-Olive Couscous

START TO FINISH: 30 minutes **MAKES:** 8 servings

- 2 cloves garlic, minced
- 1 tablespoon olive oil
- 3 cups chicken broth
- 1 cup pimiento-stuffed green olives, pitted green olives, and/or pitted ripe olives, cut up
- 1 10-ounce package quick-cooking couscous
- 3 medium zucchini, halved lengthwise and thinly sliced (about 3¾ cups)
- 2 teaspoons finely shredded lemon peel
- ¼ teaspoon freshly ground black pepper
- 4 green onions, sliced (4)
- 2 tablespoons snipped fresh parsley
  Thin strips of lemon peel (optional)
  Lemon wedges

1. In a large saucepan cook garlic in hot oil for 1 minute, stirring frequently. Add broth and olives; bring to boiling. Stir in couscous, zucchini, shredded lemon peel, and pepper. Cover; remove from heat. Let stand 5 minutes.

2. To serve, gently stir in green onions and parsley. If desired, top with thin strips of lemon peel. Serve with lemon wedges.

Per serving: 190 cal., 5 g total fat (1 g sat. fat), 0 mg chol., 762 mg sodium, 31 g carbo., 3 g fiber, 6 g pro.

Holiday Cauliflower

PREP: 25 minutes BAKE: 15 minutes MAKES: 8 servings

- 6 cups water
- 6 cups cauliflower florets (1 large head cauliflower)
- 1 4-ounce can sliced mushrooms, drained
- ¼ cup chopped green sweet pepper
- ¼ cup butter
- ⅓ cup all-purpose flour
- ¼ teaspoon salt
- 2 cups milk
- 1 cup shredded Swiss cheese (4 ounces)
- 2 tablespoons diced pimiento

1. Preheat oven to 325°F. In a large saucepan bring the water to boiling. Add cauliflower; cook for 4 to 6 minutes or until crisp-tender. Drain cauliflower; set aside.

2. For sauce, in a medium saucepan cook mushrooms and sweet pepper in hot butter until pepper is tender. Stir in flour and salt. Add the milk all at once. Cook and stir until thickened and bubbly. Remove from heat. Stir in Swiss cheese and pimiento until cheese is melted.

3. In a 1½-quart casserole layer half of the cauliflower and half of the sauce. Top with remaining cauliflower and sauce.

4. Bake, uncovered, for 15 minutes. Serve warm.

Per serving: 177 cal., 11 g total fat (7 g sat. fat), 34 mg chol., 297 mg sodium, 11 g carbo., 3 g fiber, 9 g pro.

Walnut Broccoli

START TO FINISH: 25 minutes MAKES: 6 servings

1 pound broccoli, trimmed and cut into 2-inch pieces
3 tablespoons butter
2 tablespoons fresh orange juice
½ teaspoon finely shredded orange peel (set aside)
¼ teaspoon salt
3 tablespoons chopped walnuts, pine nuts, or pecans, toasted
Orange wedges (optional)

1. Halve stem pieces of broccoli lengthwise, if desired. Place a steamer basket in a 3-quart saucepan. Add water to reach just below the bottom of the basket. Bring to boiling. Add broccoli to steamer basket. Cover and reduce heat. Steam for 8 to 10 minutes or just until stems are tender. Transfer broccoli to a serving dish.

2. Meanwhile, in a medium skillet melt butter over medium-high heat; cook and stir for 3 to 4 minutes or until medium brown in color. Carefully add orange juice and cook for 10 seconds. Remove from heat; stir in orange peel and salt. Pour over broccoli; sprinkle with walnuts. If desired, garnish with orange wedges.

Per serving: 94 cal., 8 g total fat (4 g sat. fat), 15 mg chol., 153 mg sodium, 4 g carbo., 1 g fiber, 2 g pro.

Glazed Parsnips and Carrots

START TO FINISH: 20 minutes MAKES: 6 servings

- 8 ounces parsnips, cut into thin bite-size strips (2¼ cups)
- 8 ounces carrots, cut into thin bite-size strips (2¼ cups)
- ¾ cup orange juice
- ⅓ cup dried cranberries
- ½ teaspoon ground ginger
- 2 firm ripe pears, peeled, if desired, and sliced
- ⅓ cup pecan halves
- 3 tablespoons packed brown sugar
- 2 tablespoons butter

1. In a large nonstick skillet combine parsnips, carrots, orange juice, dried cranberries, and ginger. Bring to boiling; reduce heat to medium. Cook, uncovered, for 7 to 8 minutes or until vegetables are crisp-tender and most of the liquid has evaporated, stirring occasionally.

2. Stir pears, pecans, brown sugar, and butter into mixture in skillet. Cook, uncovered, for 2 to 3 minutes more or until vegetables are glazed.

Per serving: 200 cal., 9 g total fat (3 g sat. fat), 11 mg chol., 59 mg sodium, 31 g carbo., 5 g fiber, 2 g pro.

Honey-Glazed Carrots

START TO FINISH: 30 minutes MAKES: 6 servings

    4 cups water
  1½ pounds baby carrots with tops trimmed to 2 inches, peeled or
       scrubbed, or 1½ pounds packaged peeled baby carrots
    1 tablespoon butter
    1 to 2 tablespoons honey
    ½ teaspoon finely shredded lemon peel
    ¼ teaspoon crushed red pepper
    ¼ teaspoon salt
       Crushed red pepper (optional)

1. In a large skillet bring water to boiling. Add carrots. Return to boiling; reduce heat. Cover and simmer 8 to 10 minutes or until carrots are just tender. Drain carrots. Pat dry with paper towels.

2. To glaze carrots, in the same heavy skillet combine butter, honey, lemon peel, crushed red pepper, and salt. Stir constantly over medium heat until butter is melted and mixture bubbles. Carefully add carrots. Toss gently for 2 to 3 minutes or until carrots are thoroughly coated with glaze and heated through completely.

3. To serve, transfer carrots to shallow bowl or platter. Drizzle with remaining glaze from pan. Sprinkle with additional crushed red pepper.

MAKE-AHEAD DIRECTIONS: Carrots may be cooked, cooled, covered, and refrigerated up to one day ahead. Bring to room temperature (takes about 1 hour) when ready to glaze. Heat carrots in glaze for 4 to 5 minutes.

Per serving: 75 cal., 2 g total fat (1 g sat. fat), 5 mg chol., 180 mg sodium, 14 g carbo., 3 g fiber, 1 g pro.

Carrots au Gratin

PREP: 15 minutes **COOK:** 20 minutes **MAKES:** 6 servings

- I pound carrots, sliced ½ inch thick (about 3 cups)
- ¼ cup fine dry bread crumbs
- I tablespoon butter, melted
- I 10.75-ounce can condensed cream of celery soup or reduced-fat condensed cream of celery soup
- I cup shredded cheddar cheese (4 ounces)
- I teaspoon dried parsley flakes, crushed
- ½ teaspoon dried rosemary, crushed

I. Preheat oven to 350°F. In a medium saucepan cook carrot slices, covered, in a small amount of boiling water for 10 to 12 minutes or just until tender. Drain well. Meanwhile, in a small bowl combine bread crumbs and butter; set aside.

2. In a medium bowl combine cooked carrots, soup, cheese, parsley, and rosemary. Transfer to a greased 1-quart casserole. Sprinkle with bread crumb mixture. Bake, uncovered, for 20 to 25 minutes or until heated through.

Per serving: I77 cal., II g total fat (6 g sat. fat), 3I mg chol., 598 mg sodium, I4 g carbo., 3 g fiber, 7 g pro.

Green Beans and Carrots with Citrus-Hazelnut Gremolata

START TO FINISH: 35 minutes MAKES: 6 to 8 servings

- 1 pound fresh green beans, trimmed or one 16-ounce package frozen whole green beans
- 1½ cups packaged julienned carrots
- 2 tablespoons finely chopped toasted hazelnuts (filberts)* or almonds
- 2 tablespoons snipped fresh Italian parsley
- 1½ teaspoons finely shredded orange peel
- 1 teaspoon finely shredded lemon peel
- ½ teaspoon finely shredded lime peel
- 1 tablespoon butter
- 1 tablespoon olive oil
- 1 shallot, finely chopped
- 2 cloves garlic, minced
- ¼ teaspoon salt
- ⅛ teaspoon ground black pepper

1. In a 4-quart Dutch oven cook the beans and carrots, uncovered, in enough lightly salted boiling water to cover about 10 minutes or until tender; drain and set vegetables aside.

2. Meanwhile, for gremolata, in a small bowl, stir together the nuts, parsley, orange peel, lemon peel, and lime peel; set aside.

3. In the same pan heat butter and oil over medium-high heat. Add shallot and garlic; cook and stir for 1 to 2 minutes or until shallot is tender. Add the beans, carrots, salt, and pepper. Toss to heat through. Transfer vegetable mixture to a serving dish. Sprinkle with gremolata.

*TIP: To toast and remove skins from hazelnuts (filberts), place nuts in a single layer in a shallow baking pan. Bake, uncovered, in a 350°F oven for 8 to 10 minutes or until lightly toasted, stirring twice. Turn hot hazelnuts out onto a clean kitchen towel; cool slightly. Gently roll nuts in the towel to remove skins.

Per serving: 97 cal., 6 g total fat (2 g sat. fat), 5 mg chol., 138 mg sodium, 10 g carbo., 4 g fiber, 2 g pro.

Teriyaki Green Beans with Carrots

START TO FINISH: 30 minutes MAKES: 6 to 8 servings

- 1 pound fresh green beans, cut into 1-inch pieces (4 cups)
- 3 medium carrots, cut into bite-size strips (2 cups)
- 1 tablespoon butter
- 1 teaspoon cornstarch
- 3 tablespoons bottled teriyaki sauce
- 1 tablespoon water
  Toasted sesame seeds (optional)

1. In a medium saucepan cook green beans, covered, in a small amount of boiling salted water about 10 minutes or until crisp-tender, adding carrots for the last 5 minutes of cooking. Drain; set vegetables aside.

2. In the same saucepan melt butter; stir in cornstarch. Add teriyaki sauce and the 1 tablespoon water. Cook and stir until thickened and bubbly.

3. Return vegetables to saucepan; toss gently to coat. Heat through. If desired, sprinkle with toasted sesame seeds.

Per serving: 62 cal., 2 g total fat (1 g sat. fat), 5 mg chol., 550 mg sodium, 9 g carbo., 3 g fiber, 2 g pro.

Great Greek Green Beans

PREP: 10 minutes **COOK:** 20 minutes **MAKES:** 6 servings

- ½ cup chopped onion
- 1 clove garlic, minced
- 1 tablespoon olive oil
- 1 28-ounce can diced tomatoes, undrained
- ¼ cup sliced pitted ripe olives
- 1 teaspoon dried oregano, crushed
- 1 16-ounce package frozen french-cut green beans, thawed and drained
- ½ cup crumbled feta cheese (2 ounces)

1. In a large skillet cook onion and garlic in hot oil about 5 minutes or until tender. Add undrained tomatoes, olives, and oregano. Bring to boiling; reduce heat. Boil gently, uncovered, for 10 minutes. Add beans. Return to boiling. Boil gently, uncovered, about 8 minutes or until desired consistency and beans are tender.

2. Transfer to a serving bowl; sprinkle with cheese. If desired, serve with a slotted spoon.

Per serving: 132 cal., 5 g total fat (2 g sat. fat), 8 mg chol., 419 mg sodium, 15 g carbo., 5 g fiber, 4 g pro.

Farm-Style Green Beans

START TO FINISH: 25 minutes **MAKES:** 4 servings

- 8 ounces fresh green beans
- 2 slices bacon, cut up
- 1 medium onion, thinly sliced (about 1 cup)
- ½ cup fresh sliced mushrooms
- 1½ cups chopped tomato or one 14.5-ounce can diced tomatoes, drained
- ¼ teaspoon salt*

1. Leave green beans whole or cut into 1-inch pieces. In a large saucepan cook the beans in a small amount of boiling salted water about 10 minutes or until crisp-tender; drain.

2. Meanwhile, in a large skillet cook bacon over medium heat until crisp. Remove bacon, reserving drippings. Drain bacon on paper towels; set aside. Cook onion and mushrooms in reserved drippings over medium heat until tender. Add tomato and salt. Cook, uncovered, 2 to 3 minutes or until most of the liquid is absorbed.

3. Transfer green beans to a serving bowl. Top with onion mixture and bacon.

*NOTE: Omit salt if using canned tomatoes.

Per serving: 132 cal., 9 g total fat (3 g sat. fat), 13 mg chol., 312 mg sodium, 10 g carbo., 3 g fiber, 4 g pro.

Lemon-Tarragon Asparagus Salad

PREP: 20 minutes CHILL: 2 hours MAKES: 6 to 8 servings

1½ pounds asparagus spears
1 cup sliced radishes
2 tablespoons olive oil
1 tablespoon thinly sliced green onion
2 teaspoons snipped fresh tarragon or ½ teaspoon dried tarragon, crushed
1 teaspoon finely shredded lemon peel
¼ teaspoon salt
¼ cup slivered almonds, toasted
2 tablespoons white balsamic vinegar or white wine vinegar

1. In a large saucepan bring a large amount of lightly salted water to boiling. Meanwhile, wash asparagus. Snap off and discard woody bases. Cut spears into 1-inch pieces. Add to boiling water; return to boiling. Cover and cook for 2 minutes. Drain and rinse with cold water.

2. Transfer asparagus to a salad bowl. Add radishes, olive oil, green onion, tarragon, lemon peel, and salt. Toss to combine. Cover and chill for 2 to 3 hours.

3. Just before serving, stir in the almonds and the vinegar.

Per serving: 100 cal., 8 g total fat (1 g sat. fat), 0 mg chol., 112 mg sodium, 6 g carbo., 3 g fiber, 4 g pro.

Cranberry-Broccoli Salad

PREP: 20 minutes CHILL: 1 hour MAKES: 10 to 12 servings

- 1¼ cups cranberries, chopped
- ¼ cup sugar
- 4 cups broccoli florets
- 4 cups packaged shredded cabbage with carrot (coleslaw mix)
- ½ cup chopped walnuts
- ½ cup raisins
- ⅓ cup chopped onion
- 6 slices bacon, crisp-cooked, drained, and crumbled
- 1 cup light mayonnaise dressing
- ¼ cup sugar
- 1 tablespoon vinegar

1. In a small bowl combine the cranberries and ¼ cup sugar; cover and chill in the refrigerator until serving time (berries will juice out).

2. In a very large bowl, combine broccoli, shredded cabbage, walnuts, raisins, onion, and bacon. Set aside.

3. In a small bowl combine mayonnaise, ¼ cup sugar, and vinegar; add to cabbage mixture. Toss to combine. Cover and chill in the refrigerator at least 1 hour or up to 24 hours.

4. Just before serving, gently fold in cranberry mixture.

Per serving: 229 cal., 14 g total fat (3 g sat. fat), 11 mg chol., 225 mg sodium, 26 g carbo., 3 g fiber, 4 g pro.

Nutty Apple Salad

START TO FINISH: 20 minutes **MAKES:** 8 to 10 servings

   Romaine leaves
9 cups torn mixed greens
1 small tart green apple, cored and cut into wedges
1 small red apple, cored and cut into bite-size pieces
3 tablespoons cider vinegar
3 tablespoons olive oil
¼ teaspoon ground black pepper
⅛ teaspoon salt
⅓ cup mixed nuts, toasted

1. Lay several romaine leaves on a large platter. Top with the torn greens and apples.

2. In a small screw-top jar combine cider vinegar, olive oil, pepper, and salt. Place lid on jar and shake dressing well. Drizzle dressing over salad. Sprinkle with nuts.

Per serving: 107 cal., 8 g total fat (1 g sat. fat), 0 mg chol., 43 mg sodium, 8 g carbo., 2 g fiber, 2 g pro.

Avocado, Grapefruit, and Spinach Salad

START TO FINISH: 20 minutes **MAKES:** 6 servings

- 1 6-ounce package fresh baby spinach or 8 cups fresh baby spinach and/or assorted torn greens
- 1 cup fresh raspberries
- 2 grapefruit, peeled and sectioned
- 2 avocados, peeled, pitted, and sliced
   Several dashes chili powder
- ¼ cup raspberry vinegar
- ¼ cup olive oil
- 2 teaspoons sugar (optional)

1. On a large serving platter or individual salad plates, arrange the spinach or mixed greens, raspberries, grapefruit sections, and avocado slices. Sprinkle with chili powder.

2. In a small bowl whisk together raspberry vinegar, olive oil, and, if desired, sugar. Drizzle over the salads.

Per serving: 220 cal., 19 g total fat (3 g sat. fat), 0 mg chol., 58 mg sodium, 13 g carbo., 9 g fiber, 3 g pro.

Pistachio Fig Salad

START TO FINISH: 20 minutes MAKES: 4 servings

- ¼ cup freshly squeezed orange juice (about ½ of a large orange)
- 2 tablespoons balsamic vinegar
- 1 clove garlic, minced
- 1 teaspoon hot sweet mustard
- 2 tablespoons salad oil
- 4 cups mixed baby greens (watercress, arugula, frisee, radicchio, curly endive, and edible flowers)
- 1 tart apple, cored and thinly sliced
- ½ cup crumbled Gorgonzola or other blue cheese
- ¼ cup roasted pistachio nuts

1. For dressing, in a small bowl whisk together orange juice, balsamic vinegar, garlic, and mustard; gradually whisk in oil until well blended. Set aside to mellow flavors.

2. For salad, divide greens equally among four salad plates. Add apple slices to plates. Sprinkle salad with Gorgonzola cheese and pistachio nuts. Whisk dressing and drizzle over the salads.

Per serving: 210 cal., 15 g total fat (4 g sat. fat), 13 mg chol., 252 mg sodium, 13 g carbo., 2 g fiber, 6 g pro.

Crimson Greens and Papaya

START TO FINISH: 25 minutes MAKES: 8 servings

- 1 large papaya
- 7 cups torn red-tip leaf lettuce and/or mixed salad greens
- 1 cup shredded radicchio
- ¼ cup snipped fresh cilantro
- ¼ cup salad oil
- 2 tablespoons lemon juice
- 2 tablespoons rice wine vinegar or white wine vinegar
- 1 tablespoon sugar
- ⅛ teaspoon salt
- 1 small red onion, thinly sliced and separated into rings

1. Halve, seed, peel and slice the papaya, reserving 1 tablespoon of the seeds for the dressing; set aside.

2. In a large salad bowl combine leaf lettuce, radicchio, and cilantro; toss gently to mix.

3. For dressing, in a blender or food processor combine salad oil, lemon juice, vinegar, sugar, and salt. Cover and blend or process until smooth. Add the reserved papaya seeds and blend or process until the seeds are the consistency of coarsely ground pepper. Pour dressing over salad. Toss lightly to coat. Arrange salad on plates; add papaya and onion.

Per serving: 87 cal., 7 g total fat (1 g sat. fat), 0 mg chol., 40 mg sodium, 6 g carbo., 1 g fiber, 1 g pro.

Fruit Verde

PREP: 15 minutes **CHILL:** 1 hour **MAKES:** 8 servings

1 cup honeydew melon balls or cubes
1 cup seedless green grapes
1 pear, cored and cut into ½-inch pieces
3 kiwifruits
½ cup white grape juice
½ cup loosely packed fresh mint leaves
Fresh mint leaves

1. In a large bowl combine melon, grapes, and pear. Peel and thinly slice 2 of the kiwifruits. Gently stir into melon mixture. Cover and chill until serving time.

2. For syrup, peel and cut up remaining kiwifruit. Add to blender container along with grape juice and the ½ cup mint. Cover; blend until smooth. Cover and chill for 1 hour.

3. To serve, pour syrup over chilled fruit. Toss well to combine. Garnish with additional mint, if desired.

Per serving: 68 cal., 0 g total fat (0 g sat. fat), 0 mg chol., 4 mg sodium, 16 g carbo., 1 g fiber, 1 g pro.

Broccoli Corn Bread

PREP: 10 minutes BAKE: 25 minutes MAKES: 16 servings

- 3 eggs
- 1 8.5-ounce package corn muffin mix
- 2 cups shredded cheddar cheese (8 ounces)
- 2 cups frozen chopped broccoli, thawed
- ½ cup chopped onion (1 medium)

1. Preheat oven to 350°F. Grease a 9×9×2-inch baking pan; set aside. In a large bowl beat eggs with a whisk or rotary beater; stir in corn muffin mix. Stir in cheddar cheese, broccoli, and onion. Spoon into prepared baking pan. Bake for 25 to 30 minutes or until a toothpick inserted near the center comes out clean. Serve warm.

Per serving: 138 cal., 7 g total fat (3 g sat. fat), 55 mg chol., 211 mg sodium, 12 g carbo., 1 g fiber, 6 g pro.

Green Onion Parker House Biscuits

PREP: 10 minutes BAKE: 8 minutes MAKES: 10 biscuits

    1 5.2-ounce container Boursin cheese with garlic and herb
    ¼ cup sliced green onions (2)
    1 12-ounce package (10) refrigerated biscuits
    1 egg yolk
    1 tablespoon water
    2 tablespoons grated Parmesan cheese
       Sliced green onions

1. Preheat oven to 400°F. In a small bowl, stir together Boursin cheese and the ¼ cup green onions; set aside.

2. Unwrap biscuits. Using your fingers, gently split the biscuits horizontally. Place the biscuit bottoms on a greased cookie sheet. Spread about 1 tablespoon of the cheese mixture over each biscuit bottom. Replace biscuit tops.

3. In a small bowl use a fork to beat together egg yolk and the water. Brush biscuit tops with yolk mixture. Sprinkle with Parmesan cheese and additional sliced green onions. Bake for 8 to 10 minutes or until golden brown. Serve warm.

Per biscuit: 149 cal., 8 g total fat (5 g sat. fat), 23 mg chol., 394 mg sodium, 16 g carbo., 0 g fiber, 4 g pro.

Cheese-Herb Biscuits

PREP: 15 minutes BAKE: 10 minutes MAKES: 10 to 12 biscuits

    2 cups all-purpose flour
    4 teaspoons baking powder
    ½ teaspoon salt
    ¼ cup shortening
    3 ounces Gruyère cheese, shredded (¾ cup)
    2 tablespoons snipped fresh dill
    ⅔ cup milk

1. Preheat oven to 450°F. In a large bowl stir together flour, baking powder, and salt. Using a pastry blender, cut in shortening until mixture resembles coarse crumbs. Stir in cheese and dill. Make a well in the center of the flour-cheese mixture. Add milk all at once. Using a fork, stir just until moistened.

2. On a lightly floured surface, quickly knead dough for 10 to 12 strokes or until nearly smooth. Pat dough to ½-inch thickness. Cut dough with a floured 2½-inch scalloped round cutter. Place biscuits on an ungreased baking sheet. Bake for 10 to 12 minutes or until golden. Serve warm.

Per biscuit: 174 cal., 8 g total fat (3 g sat. fat), 10 mg chol., 311 mg sodium, 19 g carbo., 1 g fiber, 5 g pro.

203

8 Sweets and Desserts

And now for the best part of the meal—dessert! A little bit of sugar and spice will finish dinner right.

Easy Crème de Menthe Cake

PREP: 25 minutes **BAKE:** according to package directions
COOL: 10 minutes **MAKES:** 12 servings

- 1 package 2-layer-size chocolate cake mix
- ¼ cup crème de menthe
- ½ cup fudge ice cream topping
- 1 16-ounce can vanilla frosting
- 1 tablespoon crème de menthe
  Few drops green food coloring (optional)
  Layered chocolate-mint candies, coarsely chopped (optional)

1. Preheat oven to 350°F. Grease and lightly flour two 8×1½- or 9×1½-inch round cake pans; set aside.

2. Prepare cake mix according to package directions, except substitute the ¼ cup crème de menthe for ¼ cup of the water. Divide batter evenly between prepared pans.

3. Bake according to package directions. Cool in pans on wire racks for 10 minutes. Remove cake layers from pans; cool on wire racks. In small saucepan, heat the fudge topping just until spreadable.

4. To assemble, place one cake layer on serving plate. Spread with fudge topping. Top with remaining cake layer.

5. In a medium bowl combine vanilla frosting and the 1 tablespoon crème de menthe. If desired, tint with green food coloring. Spread frosting over top and side of cake. If desired, garnish with chocolate-mint candies.

Per serving: 435 cal., 19 g total fat (4 g sat. fat), 35 mg chol., 383 mg sodium, 66 g carbo., 1 g fiber, 3 g pro.

Pecan Streusel Dessert

PREP: 20 minutes **BAKE:** 35 minutes **COOL:** 15 minutes
MAKES: 15 servings

- 1 cup chopped pecans
- ⅔ cup packed brown sugar
- 2 tablespoons butter, melted
- 1½ teaspoons ground cinnamon
- 1 26.5-ounce package cinnamon streusel coffee cake mix
- ½ cup dairy sour cream

1. Preheat oven to 350°F. Grease and flour a 13×9×2-inch baking pan; set aside. For topping, in a small bowl stir together pecans, brown sugar, butter, and cinnamon.

2. Prepare the coffee cake mix according to the package directions, except stir sour cream into prepared batter. Spread half of the batter (about 3 cups) into the prepared pan. Sprinkle batter with the streusel mix from the package of coffee cake mix. Carefully spread with the remaining batter. Sprinkle with the topping.

3. Bake in the preheated oven for 35 to 40 minutes or until a toothpick inserted near center comes out clean. Cool slightly in pan.

4. Meanwhile, prepare glaze from the coffee cake mix according to package directions. Drizzle glaze over warm cake.

Per serving: 395 cal., 20 g total fat (5 g sat. fat), 50 mg chol., 243 mg sodium, 50 g carbo., 1 g fiber, 4 g pro.

Hazelnut Cream Cassata

PREP: 30 minutes **BAKE:** 15 minutes **CHILL:** up to 24 hours
MAKES: 12 servings

  - 1 package 2-layer-size white or lemon cake mix
  - 1 tablespoon finely shredded lemon peel (only if using white cake mix)
  - ⅓ cup chocolate-hazelnut spread
  - ⅓ cup ricotta cheese
  - ⅓ cup seedless red raspberry jam
  - 1½ cups whipping cream
  - 2 tablespoons powdered sugar
    Halved hazelnuts, toasted (see tip, page 167)

1. Preheat oven to 350°F. Grease and flour three 9×1½-inch-round cake pans. Set aside.

2. Prepare cake mix according to package directions. (If using white cake mix, stir in lemon peel.) Divide batter among prepared cake pans. Bake about 15 minutes or until toothpick inserted near center comes out clean. Cool in pans on wire racks for 10 minutes. Remove cake layers from pans. Cool on wire racks.

3. In a small bowl stir together chocolate-hazelnut spread and ricotta cheese. Place one cake layer on serving platter. Spread top with half of the jam. Spread half of the chocolate mixture over jam. Top with another cake layer. Spread top with remaining jam and remaining chocolate mixture. Top with remaining cake layer.

4. In a chilled medium bowl beat whipping cream and powdered sugar with chilled beaters of electric mixer on medium speed just until stiff peaks form (tips stand straight). Spread whipped cream over top and side of cake. Top with hazelnuts. If desired, cover and chill for up to 4 hours.

TIP: If you have only two 9-inch cake pans, cover and chill one-third of the batter and bake it after the other layers are out of the pans.

Per serving: 413 cal., 23 g total fat (10 g sat. fat), 45 mg chol., 310 mg sodium, 47 g carbo., 1 g fiber, 5 g pro.

Candy Bar Pie

PREP: 30 minutes **BAKE:** 10 minutes **COOL:** 30 minutes
FREEZE: 5 hours **MAKES:** 8 servings

  1½ cups coarsely ground walnuts (6 ounces)
  3 tablespoons butter, melted
  2 tablespoons sugar
  6 1- to 1½-ounce bars milk chocolate with almonds, chopped
  15 large marshmallows or 1½ cups tiny marshmallows
  ½ cup milk
  1 cup whipping cream
  ½ teaspoon vanilla
    Whipped cream (optional)
    Coarsely chopped milk chocolate bars with almonds (optional)

1. Preheat oven to 325°F. In a medium mixing bowl combine ground walnuts, melted butter and sugar. Press onto the bottom and side of a 9-inch pie plate to form a firm, even crust. Bake about 10 minutes or until edge is golden brown. Cool on a wire rack.

2. For filling, in a medium saucepan combine the 6 chopped chocolate bars, the marshmallows, and milk. Heat and stir over medium-low heat until chocolate is melted. Remove from heat. Let the chocolate mixture stand until cooled to room temperature. Chill a large mixing bowl and beaters.

3. In the chilled mixing bowl beat the 1 cup cream and the vanilla with an electric mixer on medium speed until soft peaks form (tips curl).

4. Fold whipped cream mixture into cooled chocolate mixture. Spoon chocolate mixture into prepared crust. Cover and freeze about 5 hours or until firm.

5. To serve, remove from the freezer and let stand about 10 minutes before cutting into wedges.* If desired, garnish with additional whipped cream and chopped chocolate bars.

*NOTE: For easier serving, set the pie on a warm, damp towel for a couple of minutes before cutting the first wedge.

Per serving: 440 cal., 36 g total fat (12 g sat. fat), 46 mg chol., 92 mg sodium, 27 g carbo., 2 g fiber, 6 g pro.

Chocolate Raspberry Cloud

PREP: 30 minutes **CHILL:** 13 hours **MAKES:** 10 servings

- 1¼ cups crushed chocolate wafers (about 20)
- ¼ cup butter, melted
- 2 cups whipping cream
- ½ cup sugar
- 1 teaspoon vanilla
- ½ cup raspberry syrup
  Several drops red food coloring (optional)
- 1 9-ounce package chocolate wafers
  Whipped cream (optional)
  Fresh raspberries (optional)

1. Combine crushed chocolate wafers and melted butter. Spread evenly in bottom and up side of a 9-inch pie plate. Press to form a firm crust. Chill, covered, in the refrigerator about 1 hour.

2. Meanwhile, beat whipping cream, sugar, and vanilla until stiff peaks form (tips stand straight). Fold in raspberry syrup and food coloring, if desired. Spread about ¾ cup raspberry mixture into prepared crust. Top with chocolate wafers (about 13), overlapping slightly. Repeat layers twice; spread top with remaining raspberry mixture. Cover loosely; chill in the refrigerator at least 12 hours. If desired, before serving, dollop additional whipped cream on pie and garnish with fresh raspberries.

Per serving: 458 cal., 27 g total fat (16 g sat. fat), 82 mg chol., 343 mg sodium, 50 g carbo., 1 g fiber, 3 g pro.

Peach Kuchen

PREP: 30 minutes **BAKE:** 30 minutes **STAND:** 15 minutes
MAKES: 10 to 12 servings

- 1½ cups all-purpose flour
- ¾ cup granulated sugar
- 2 teaspoons baking powder
- ¼ teaspoon salt
- ¼ teaspoon ground nutmeg or mace
- ¼ cup butter
- ½ cup milk
- 1 egg, beaten
- 2 cups sliced fresh or unsweetened frozen peaches, thawed and well drained on paper towels
- ⅓ cup packed brown sugar
- 1 tablespoon light corn syrup
- 1 tablespoon butter
- 1 teaspoon lemon juice
- ¼ teaspoon ground nutmeg or mace

1. Preheat oven to 350°F. Grease and flour an 11-inch tart pan with a removable bottom. Set aside.

2. In a medium bowl stir together the flour, granulated sugar, baking powder, salt and the ¼ teaspoon nutmeg. Using a pastry blender or 2 knives, cut in the ¼ cup butter until mixture resembles coarse crumbs. Make a well in the center; add milk and egg all at once to the flour mixture. Stir just until moistened and dough clings together (batter should be lumpy).

3. Spread batter into the prepared pan. Halve any large slices of frozen peaches. Arrange peach slices on top in a single layer. Set aside.

4. In a small saucepan combine brown sugar, corn syrup, the 1 tablespoon butter, lemon juice and the ¼ teaspoon nutmeg or mace. Bring to boiling. Quickly drizzle over peach slices.

5. Bake for 30 to 35 minutes or until a toothpick inserted in the center comes out clean. Cool kuchen in pan on a wire rack for 15 minutes. Remove the sides of the pan. Serve warm.

Per serving: 240 cal., 7 g total fat (4 g sat. fat), 39 mg chol., 218 mg sodium, 42 g carbo., 1 g fiber, 3 g pro.

Easy Cream Cheese Tart

PREP: 40 minutes **BAKE:** 20 minutes **COOL:** 1 hour
CHILL: 4 hours **MAKES:** 8 to 10 servings

½ of a 15-ounce package rolled refrigerated unbaked piecrust (1 crust)
2 8-ounce packages cream cheese, softened
⅓ cup sugar
1 tablespoon all-purpose flour
1 teaspoon vanilla
2 tablespoons lemon juice, amaretto, brandy, or rum
2 eggs, slightly beaten
1 teaspoon finely shredded lemon peel
⅓ cup sliced almonds
   Apricot, peach, plum, or cherry preserves
   Sweetened Whipped Cream (see recipe, right) (optional)
   Fresh raspberries, peach slices, or nectarine slices (optional)

1. Preheat oven to 450°F. Let piecrust stand at room temperature for 15 minutes before unrolling. Place piecrust circle in a 10-inch tart pan with a removable bottom or ease into a 9-inch pie plate. Press piecrust circle onto bottom and up sides of tart pan, if using; trim edges, if necessary. If using a pie plate, turn under edges and crimp as desired.

Line pastry with a double thickness of foil. Bake for 8 minutes. Remove foil; bake 5 to 6 minutes more or until lightly browned. Reduce oven temperature to 350°F.

2. Meanwhile, for filling, in a large mixing bowl beat cream cheese, sugar, flour, and vanilla with an electric mixer until combined. Beat in lemon juice until smooth. Stir in eggs and lemon peel.

3. Pour filling into pastry shell. Sprinkle with sliced almonds. Bake for 20 to 25 minutes or until center appears nearly set when gently shaken. Cool for 1 hour on a wire rack. If using the tart pan, carefully remove the sides. Cover and chill for 4 to 24 hours.

4. To serve, cut into wedges. Spoon preserves over each serving. If you like, serve with Sweetened Whipped Cream and fresh fruit.

Per serving: 431 cal., 31 g total fat (16 g sat. fat), 120 mg chol., 287 mg sodium, 31 g carbo., 1 g fiber, 8 g pro.

SWEETENED WHIPPED CREAM: In a chilled small mixing bowl combine 1 cup whipping cream, 2 tablespoons sugar and ½ teaspoon vanilla. Beat with chilled beaters of an electric mixer on medium speed until soft peaks form.

Chocolate Pavlova

PREP: 30 minutes BAKE: 40 minutes STAND: 30 minutes
CHILL: 30 to 60 minutes MAKES: 8 to 10 servings

3	egg whites
1	tablespoon raspberry vinegar or red wine vinegar
1½	teaspoons vanilla
⅛	teaspoon salt
⅛	teaspoon cream of tartar
1	cup sugar
¼	cup unsweetened cocoa powder
1½	teaspoons cornstarch
1	cup whipping cream
1	tablespoon sugar
3	cups peeled and cut up kiwi fruit, fresh raspberries, and/or seeded, peeled and sliced mango

1. Preheat oven to 350°F. Line a baking sheet with a piece of parchment paper. Use a pencil to draw or trace an 8-inch circle on the paper. Turn paper pencil-side down; set aside.

2. In a large mixing bowl beat the egg whites, vinegar, vanilla, salt, and cream of tartar with an electric mixer on medium to high speed until egg whites are foamy. In a small bowl stir together 1 cup sugar, cocoa powder, and cornstarch. Continue to beat egg white mixture on medium to high speed while gradually adding the sugar mixture. Beat until stiff, glossy peaks form (tips stand straight).

3. Spoon egg white mixture onto prepared baking sheet, spreading to fill the circle, and smoothing with a spatula to make a flat top.

4. Bake for 10 minutes. Reduce oven temperature to 300°F. Bake for 30 minutes more or until meringue is cracked on top. Turn oven off. Let stand in the oven for 30 minutes. Remove and cool completely on a wire rack.

5. In a clean large bowl beat the whipping cream and 1 tablespoon sugar with an electric mixer on medium speed or with a whisk until stiff peaks form. Place meringue on a serving platter. Top with the whipped cream, spreading evenly to within ½ inch of the edges. Arrange fruit on top of cream. Cover loosely and chill 30 to 60 minutes. To serve, slice into wedges.

Per serving: 265 cal., 12 g total fat (7 g sat. fat), 41 mg chol., 70 mg sodium, 38 g carbo., 2 g fiber, 3 g pro.

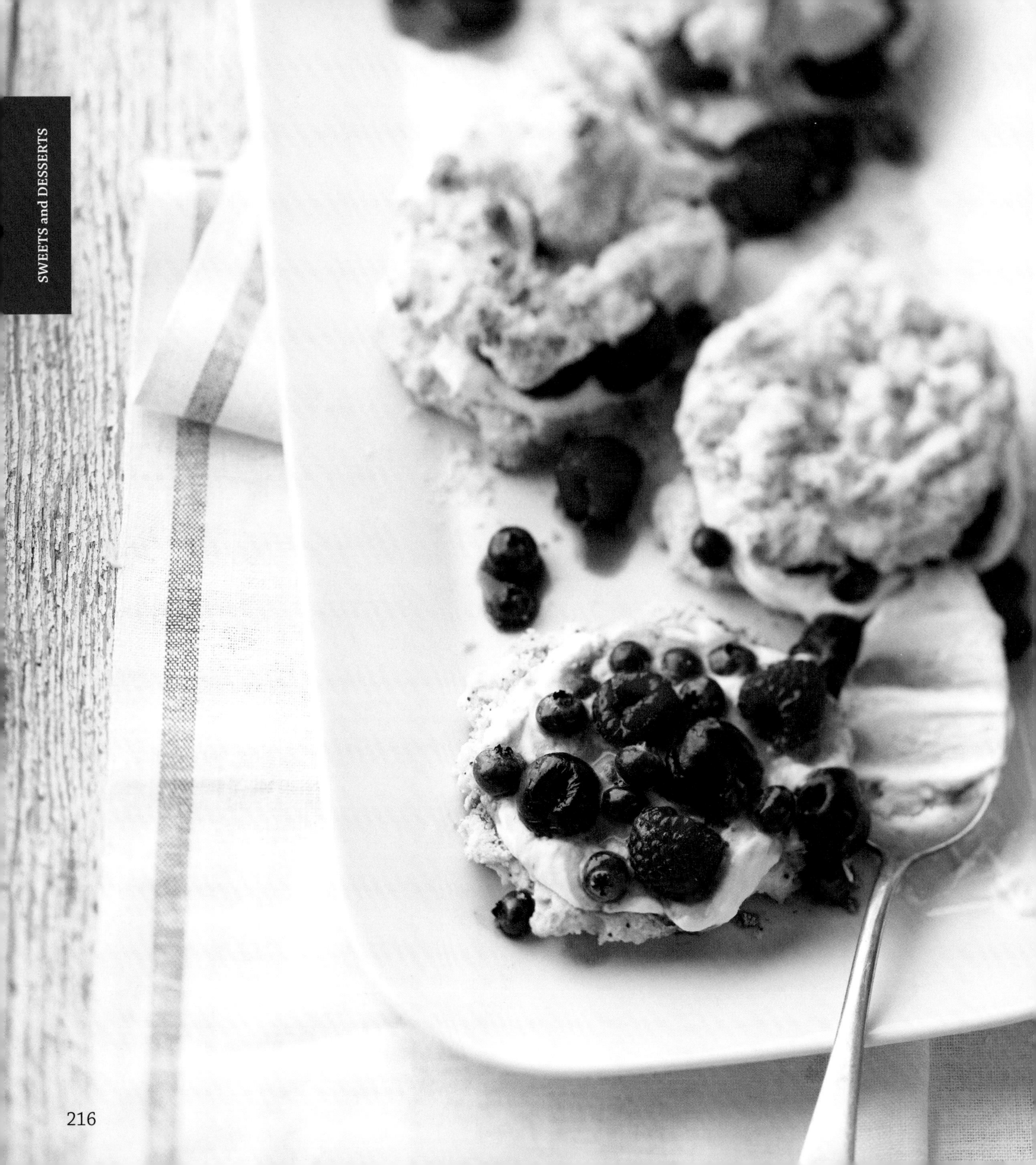

Cherry-Berry Rich Shortcakes

PREP: 30 minutes **BAKE:** 10 minutes **COOL:** 5 minutes
MAKES: 6 servings

- 2 cups fresh or frozen unsweetened blueberries, thawed
- 1 cup fresh or frozen unsweetened raspberries, thawed, or sliced strawberries
- 1 cup fresh or frozen unsweetened pitted sweet cherries, thawed
- ¼ cup sugar
- 3 cups packaged biscuit mix
- ¼ teaspoon ground nutmeg or ground cinnamon
- ¼ cup cold butter
- ⅔ cup half-and-half, light cream, or whole milk
  Sugar
- 1 cup whipping cream
- 2 tablespoons sugar
- ½ teaspoon vanilla

1. Preheat oven to 425°F. In a large bowl, combine blueberries, raspberries, cherries and ¼ cup sugar; set aside.

2. For shortcake: In a large bowl stir together biscuit mix and nutmeg. Use a pastry blender to cut butter into biscuit mixture until mixture resembles coarse crumbs. Make a well in the center of the mixture. Add half-and-half all at once. Using a fork, stir just until moistened. Drop dough into 6 mounds on an ungreased baking sheet; flatten each mound with the back of a spoon until about ¾-inch thick. Lightly sprinkle each mound with additional sugar.

3. Bake for 10 to 12 minutes or until golden. Cool on a wire rack for 5 minutes.

4. Meanwhile, in a chilled medium bowl beat whipping cream, 2 tablespoons sugar, and vanilla with an electric mixer with chilled beaters on medium speed until soft peaks form.

5. To serve, split warm shortcakes in half horizontally. Using a wide spatula, carefully lift off the top layer. Place bottom layers in 6 shallow dessert dishes. Spoon whipped cream over the bottom layer. Spoon fruit mixture over whipped cream. Carefully replace the top layers. Serve immediately.

Per serving: 604 cal., 35 g total fat (18 g sat. fat), 86 mg chol., 855 mg sodium, 67 g carbo., 4 g fiber, 7 g pro.

Chocolate Cherry Mini Cheesecakes

PREP: 30 minutes **BAKE:** 20 minutes **COOL:** 5 minutes
CHILL: 4 hours **MAKES:** 12 mini cheesecakes

- 12 vanilla wafers
- 1 8-ounce package cream cheese, softened
- 1 3-ounce package cream cheese, softened
- 3 ounces bittersweet or semisweet chocolate, melted and cooled
- ⅔ cup sugar
- 2 egg yolks
- 3 tablespoons chocolate liqueur, apricot brandy or milk
- 1 tablespoon milk
- 1½ teaspoons vanilla
- ⅓ cup finely chopped dried cherries or dried apricots
  Chocolate shavings and/or small whole or sliced strawberries (optional)

1. Preheat oven to 350°F. Line twelve 2½-inch muffin cups with foil bake cups. Place 1 wafer in the bottom of each muffin cup. Set aside.

2. For filling, in a medium mixing bowl beat cream cheese and chocolate with an electric mixer until combined. Beat in sugar, egg yolks, liqueur, milk, and vanilla just until combined (do not overbeat). Stir in dried cherries. Spoon filling into each prepared cup.

3. Bake about 20 minutes or until set. Cool in muffin pan on a wire rack for 5 minutes. (Centers may dip slightly as they cool.) Remove cheesecakes from pans. Cool on a wire rack for 1 hour. Cover and chill for 4 to 24 hours.

4. If desired, garnish with chocolate shavings or strawberries before serving.

Per serving: 227 cal., 13 g total fat (8 g sat. fat), 63 mg chol., 98 mg sodium, 24 g carbo., 1 g fiber, 3 g pro.

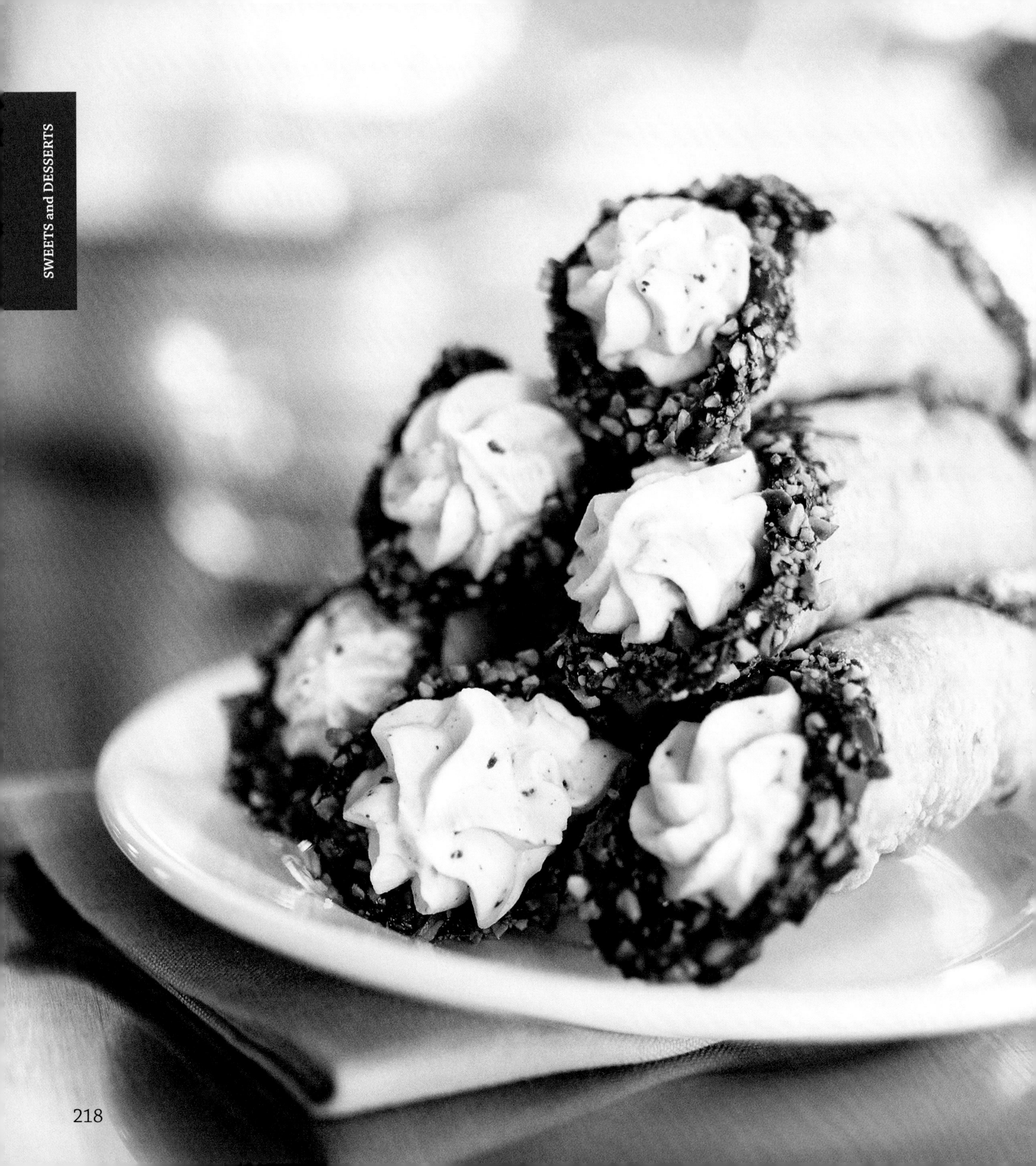

Cannoli

PREP: 25 minutes STAND: 45 minutes CHILL: up to 8 hours
MAKES: 12 servings

I I5-ounce carton ricotta cheese
¾ cup powdered sugar
I teaspoon vanilla
I ounce bittersweet or semisweet chocolate, grated
4 ounces bittersweet or semisweet chocolate, chopped
I tablespoon shortening
I2 to I4 purchased cannoli shells
¾ cup finely chopped pistachio nuts
I cup whipping cream

I. For filling, in a medium bowl stir together ricotta cheese, powdered sugar, and vanilla until almost smooth. Stir in grated chocolate. Cover and chill up to 6 hours.

2. Meanwhile, in a small saucepan heat and stir chopped chocolate and the shortening over low heat until melted. Remove from heat. Transfer to a small bowl. Dip both ends of the cannoli shells in chocolate, letting excess drip off. Sprinkle chocolate ends with pistachio nuts. Place on a wire rack placed over waxed paper to dry (about 45 minutes).

3. When chocolate is dry, in a medium bowl beat whipping cream with an electric mixer on medium speed or with a wire whisk until stiff peaks form. Fold into the ricotta mixture. Spoon filling into a decorating bag fitted with a large round or open star tip (or spoon into a resealable plastic bag, seal bag, and snip off a small corner of the bag). Pipe filling into shells. Cover and chill up to 2 hours.

MAKE-AHEAD DIRECTIONS: You can store the dipped cannoli shells in chocolate (Step 2) in an airtight container for up to 3 days.

Per serving: 388 cal., 29 g total fat (I2 g sat. fat), 45 mg chol., 48 mg sodium, 28 g carbo., 3 g fiber, 9 g pro.

CHOCOLATE CANNOLI: Prepare Cannoli as directed, except stir ¼ cup unsweetened cocoa powder in with the ricotta cheese.

Chocolate-Kissed Date Puffs

PREP: 35 minutes BAKE: 12 minutes MAKES: 18 puffs

I egg
I tablespoon water
I I7.3-ounce package frozen puff pastry (2 sheets), thawed
I I3-ounce jar chocolate-hazelnut spread
½ cup coarsely chopped hazelnuts (filberts), toasted
⅓ cup chopped pitted dates
⅓ cup large milk chocolate pieces

I. Preheat oven to 400° F. Lightly grease 2 cookie sheets; set aside. In a small bowl beat together egg and the 1 tablespoon water; set aside.

2. Unfold one pastry sheet on a lightly floured surface. Roll to a 12-inch square. Cut into nine 4-inch squares. Spread the center of each square with about 1 tablespoon of the chocolate-hazelnut spread, leaving a 1-inch border around the edge. Divide half of the hazelnuts, dates, and chocolate pieces evenly among the prepared pastry squares, placing atop spread. Brush edges of squares with egg mixture. Fold each to form a triangle and crimp edges with a fork to seal.

3. Prick tops with the fork. Transfer to one of the prepared cookie sheets. Brush with egg mixture. Bake for 12 to 15 minutes or until golden. Repeat with remaining ingredients. Cool slightly on wire racks. Serve warm.

Per serving: 282 cal., I8 g total fat (I g sat. fat), I3 mg chol., I28 mg sodium, 27 g carbo., I g fiber, 4 g pro.

Chocolate Éclairs

PREP: 35 minutes **BAKE:** 33 minutes **CHILL:** up to 2 hours
MAKES: 12 éclairs

1 cup all-purpose flour
3 tablespoons unsweetened cocoa powder
2 tablespoons sugar
1 cup water
½ cup butter
¼ teaspoon salt
4 eggs
2 cups whipping cream
Purchased hot fudge sauce (optional)
Powdered sugar (optional)

1. Preheat oven to 400°F. Grease a cookie sheet; set aside. Stir together flour, cocoa powder, and sugar. In a saucepan bring water, butter, and salt to boiling; stir until butter melts. Add flour mixture all at once to boiling mixture, stirring vigorously. Cook and stir until mixture forms a ball. Cool 10 minutes.

2. Add eggs, one at a time, beating with a wooden spoon about 1 minute after each addition or until smooth.

3. Spoon the batter into a pastry bag fitted with a large plain round tip (½- to 1-inch opening). Pipe strips of batter (measuring about 4 inches long, 1 inch wide, and ¾ inch high) 3 inches apart onto prepared cookie sheet.

4. Bake for 33 to 35 minutes or until puffy, golden and firm to the touch. Remove from cookie sheet; cool on a wire rack.

5. Up to 2 hours before serving, in a large bowl beat cream just until stiff peaks form (do not overbeat). Cut off tops of éclairs. Remove soft dough from inside. Pipe whipped cream into éclairs. Replace tops. Chill until serving time. If desired, top with fudge sauce and dust with powdered sugar.

Per serving: 361 cal., 27 g total fat (16 g sat. fat), 143 mg chol., 171 mg sodium, 27 g carbo., 10 g fiber, 5 g pro.

Chocolate-Coconut Bars

PREP: 25 minutes **BAKE:** 45 minutes **MAKES:** 42 bars

  1¼ cups sugar
  3 eggs
  1 tablespoon all-purpose flour
  ½ teaspoon baking powder
  1 teaspoon vanilla
  1 7-ounce bag shredded coconut
  1 4-ounce package sweet baking chocolate
  ⅔ cup butter
  ½ cup packed brown sugar
  1 cup all-purpose flour
  ¼ teaspoon salt
  1 cup chopped almonds, toasted (see tip, page 167)

1. Preheat oven to 325°F. Line a 13×9×2-inch baking pan with foil, extending foil over edges of pan. Grease foil; set pan aside.

2. In a medium bowl whisk together ½ cup of the granulated sugar, 1 egg, 1 tablespoon all-purpose flour, the baking powder, and ½ teaspoon of the vanilla. Stir in coconut. Set aside.

3. In a large microwave-safe bowl combine chocolate and butter. Cover bowl with plastic wrap, turning back one section to vent. Microwave on 100 percent power (high setting) about 1½ minutes or until almost melted; stir until smooth. Using a wooden spoon, stir in remaining ¾ cup granulated sugar, brown sugar, 2 eggs, and ½ teaspoon vanilla until smooth. Stir in 1 cup flour and salt. Spread evenly in prepared pan. Sprinkle with almonds.

4. Spread coconut mixture evenly over chocolate layer. Bake for 45 to 50 minutes or until golden brown and just set in middle. If necessary to prevent overbrowning, cover with foil for the last 10 minutes of baking. Cool completely in pan on a wire rack.

5. To cut, lift bars out of pan with foil. Peel off foil and cut into bars.

MAKE-AHEAD DIRECTIONS: Prepare and bake as directed. Cover and freeze for up to 1 week. Thaw at room temperature.

Per serving: 125 cal., 7 g total fat (4 g sat. fat), 23 mg chol., 45 mg sodium, 14 g carbo., 1 g fiber, 2 g pro.

Quick Toffee Delight

PREP: 10 minutes **BAKE:** 2 minutes **CHILL:** 15 minutes
MAKES: 20 pieces

Nonstick cooking spray
12 graham cracker squares
24 vanilla caramels, unwrapped
2 tablespoons milk or water
1 cup chopped pecans
2 cups dark chocolate pieces or semisweet chocolate pieces

1. Preheat oven to 300°F. Line a 13×9×2-inch baking pan with foil. Lightly coat foil with cooking spray. Cover bottom of pan with a single layer of graham crackers, breaking crackers as needed to fit. Set aside.

2. In a medium microwave-safe bowl combine caramels and milk. Microwave, uncovered, on 100 percent power (high setting) for 2 to 3 minutes or until caramels are melted, stirring once. Quickly pour caramel mixture over graham crackers.

3. Sprinkle pecans over warm caramel layer. With a rubber spatula, lightly press pecans into caramel. Sprinkle chocolate pieces over top.

4. Bake about 2 minutes or until chocolate pieces soften (they will still hold their shape). Spread softened pieces with a knife or metal spatula to cover caramel evenly. Chill about 15 minutes or until firm. Use foil to lift toffee out of pan. Remove foil from toffee. On a cutting board, cut or break into pieces.

Per piece: 174 cal., 10 g total fat (3 g sat. fat), 0 mg chol., 56 mg sodium, 24 g carbo., 2 g fiber, 2 g pro.

Peppermint Thins

START TO FINISH: 35 minutes **MAKES:** 40 cookies

24 ounces vanilla candy coating, chopped
3 tablespoons shortening
⅛ teaspoon peppermint oil or peppermint candy flavoring
1 9-ounce package chocolate wafer cookies or 40 chocolate graham cracker squares
¼ cup coarsely crushed peppermint candy canes*

1. In a heavy medium saucepan combine candy coating and shortening. Cook and stir over low heat until melted. Stir in peppermint oil. Keep warm over low heat, stirring occasionally.

2. Dip one cookie at a time into the melted candy coating mixture. Remove with a fork and place on wire rack. While coating is still wet, sprinkle with crushed candy canes. If necessary, chill dipped cookies in refrigerator to set.

*****NOTE:** To crush candy canes, place candy canes in a heavy plastic bag. Crush bag lightly with meat mallet. Empty bag of crushed candy into a fine wire mesh strainer. Shake strainer over sink to remove candy dust.

Per cookie: 140 cal., 7 g total fat (5 g sat. fat), 1 mg chol., 50 mg sodium, 17 g carbo., 0 g fiber, 1 g pro.

No-Bake Orange Balls

PREP: 40 minutes STAND: 2 hours MAKES: 40 balls

- 2 cups finely crushed, crisp unfrosted sugar cookies (about 8 ounces)
- 1 cup toasted hazelnuts (filberts), almonds, or pecans, finely chopped
- 1 cup powdered sugar
- ¼ cup light-color corn syrup
- 2 tablespoons orange, coffee, or almond liqueur
- 2 tablespoons butter (no substitutes), melted
- ⅓ cup powdered sugar
- 2 teaspoons orange edible glitter (optional)

1. Combine crushed cookies, nuts, the 1 cup powdered sugar, corn syrup, liqueur, and butter in a mixing bowl; stir with a wooden spoon until well-mixed.

2. Shape mixture into 1-inch balls. Combine the ⅓ cup powdered sugar and, if desired, edible glitter. Roll balls in powdered sugar mixture; cover. Let stand 2 hours. Roll balls again in powdered sugar mixture before serving. Chill or freeze for longer storage.

Per serving: 64 cal., 3 g total fat (1 g sat. fat), 2 mg chol., 29 mg sodium, 9 g carbo., 0 g fiber, 1 g pro.

Melon with Fruit Salsa

PREP: 25 minutes **CHILL:** up to 4 hours **MAKES:** 8 servings

- 2 kiwifruits, peeled and chopped
- 2 mangoes, seeded, peeled, and chopped (2 cups)
- 2 cups chopped fresh strawberries
- 1 small fresh jalapeño chile pepper, seeded and finely chopped (about 1 tablespoon) (see note, page 75)
- ¼ cup snipped fresh mint
- 2 tablespoons lime juice
- 2 tablespoons honey
- ½ cup fresh raspberries
- 8 1-inch slices quartered watermelon
- 1 pint lemon or lime sorbet or sherbet

1. In a large bowl combine kiwifruits, mangoes, strawberries, jalapeño pepper, mint, lime juice, and honey. Gently stir in raspberries. Serve immediately or cover and chill up to 4 hours. Serve over watermelon quarters with sorbet.

Per serving: 220 cal., 1 g total fat (0 g sat. fat), 0 mg chol., 10 mg sodium, 55 g carbo., 4 g dietary fiber, 3 g protein.

Frozen Berry-Melon Pops

PREP: 20 minutes FREEZE: overnight MAKES: 8 servings

2½ cups cubed, seeded watermelon, cantaloupe, or honeydew melon
½ cup fresh or frozen raspberries, thawed
¼ cup sugar
5 teaspoons lemon juice
1 tablespoon light-colored corn syrup

1. In a blender combine melon, berries, sugar, lemon juice and corn syrup; cover and blend until smooth. Press fruit mixture through a fine-mesh strainer over a bowl to extract juices. Discard solids. Pour mixture into 3-ounce paper or plastic drink cups or pop molds. Cover cups with foil; cut a slit in the foil and insert wooden sticks.

2. Freeze several hours or overnight until pops are firm. To serve, remove from cups or molds.

Per serving: 50 cal., 0 g total fat (0 g sat. fat), 0 mg chol., 4 mg sodium, 12 g carbo., 1 g fiber, 0 g pro.

Ginger Peach Freeze

PREP: 10 minutes FREEZE: 3 hours MAKES: 8 servings

1 cup water
1 cup sugar
3 tablespoons lemon juice
¼ teaspoon ground ginger
1 16-ounce package frozen unsweetened peach slices
Fresh peach slices (optional)

1. In a medium saucepan combine water, sugar, lemon juice, and ginger. Bring to boiling. Remove from heat; add frozen peaches. Let stand about 30 minutes or until peaches are thawed and mixture has cooled.

2. Add peach mixture, half at a time, to a blender. Cover and blend until smooth. Transfer blended mixture to a 2-quart rectangular baking dish. Cover and freeze for 3 to 4 hours. Break up mixture with a fork; spoon into dessert dishes. Top with fresh peach slices.

Per serving: 119 cal., 0 g total fat (0 g sat. fat), 0 mg chol., 1 mg sodium, 31 g carbo., 1 g fiber, 0 g pro.

231

INDEX

METRIC INFORMATION

The charts on this page provide a guide for converting measurements from the U.S. customary system, which is used throughout this book, to the metric system.

Product Differences

Most of the ingredients called for in the recipes in this book are available in most countries. However, some are known
by different names. Here are some common American
ingredients and their possible counterparts:

- Sugar (white) is granulated, fine granulated, or castor sugar.
- Powdered sugar is icing sugar.
- All-purpose flour is enriched, bleached or unbleached white household flour. When self-rising flour is used in place of all-purpose flour in a recipe that calls for leavening, omit the leavening agent (baking soda or baking powder) and salt.
- Light-colored corn syrup is golden syrup.
- Cornstarch is cornflour.
- Baking soda is bicarbonate of soda.
- Vanilla or vanilla extract is vanilla essence.
- Green, red, or yellow sweet peppers are capsicums or bell peppers.
- Golden raisins are sultanas.

Volume and Weight

The United States traditionally uses cup measures for liquid and solid ingredients. The chart below shows the approximate imperial and metric equivalents. If you are accustomed to weighing solid ingredients, the following approximate equivalents will be helpful.

- 1 cup butter, castor sugar, or rice = 8 ounces = ½ pound = 250 grams
- 1 cup flour = 4 ounces = ¼ pound = 125 grams
- 1 cup icing sugar = 5 ounces = 150 grams

Canadian and U.S. volume for a cup measure is 8 fluid ounces (237 ml), but the standard metric equivalent is 250 ml.

1 British imperial cup is 10 fluid ounces.

In Australia, 1 tablespoon equals 20 ml, and there are 4 teaspoons in the Australian tablespoon.

Spoon measures are used for smaller amounts of ingredients. Although the size of the tablespoon varies slightly in different countries, for practical purposes and for recipes in this book, a straight substitution is all that's necessary. Measurements made using cups or spoons always should be level unless stated otherwise.

Common Weight Range Replacements

IMPERIAL / U.S.	METRIC
½ ounce	15 g
1 ounce	25 g or 30 g
4 ounces (¼ pound)	115 g or 125 g
8 ounces (½ pound)	225 g or 250 g
16 ounces (1 pound)	450 g or 500 g
1¼ pounds	625 g
1½ pounds	750 g
2 pounds or 2¼ pounds	1,000 g or 1 Kg

Oven Temperature Equivalents

FAHRENHEIT SETTING	CELSIUS SETTING*	GAS SETTING
300°F	150°C	Gas Mark 2 (very low)
325°F	160°C	Gas Mark 3 (low)
350°F	180°C	Gas Mark 4 (moderate)
375°F	190°C	Gas Mark 5 (moderate)
400°F	200°C	Gas Mark 6 (hot)
425°F	220°C	Gas Mark 7 (hot)
450°F	230°C	Gas Mark 8 (very hot)
475°F	240°C	Gas Mark 9 (very hot)
500°F	260°C	Gas Mark 10 (extremely hot)
Broil	Broil	Grill

*Electric and gas ovens may be calibrated using celsius.
However, for an electric oven, increase celsius setting
10 to 20 degrees when cooking above 160°C. For convection or forced air ovens (gas or electric) lower the temperature setting 25°F/10°C when cooking at all heat levels.

Baking Pan Sizes

IMPERIAL / U.S.	METRIC
9×1½-inch round cake pan	22- or 23×4-cm (1.5 L)
9×1½-inch pie plate	22- or 23×4-cm (1 L)
8×8×2-inch square cake pan	20×5-cm (2 L)
9×9×2-inch square cake pan	22- or 23×4.5-cm (2.5 L)
11×7×1½-inch baking pan	28×17×4-cm (2 L)
2-quart rectangular baking pan	30×19×4.5-cm (3 L)
13×9×2-inch baking pan	34×22×4.5-cm (3.5 L)
15×10×1-inch jelly roll pan	40×25×2-cm
9×5×3-inch loaf pan	23×13×8-cm (2 L)
2-quart casserole	2 L

U.S. / Standard Metric Equivalents

⅛ teaspoon = 0.5 ml	
¼ teaspoon = 1 ml	
½ teaspoon = 2 ml	
1 teaspoon = 5 ml	
1 tablespoon = 15 ml	
2 tablespoons = 25 ml	
¼ cup = 2 fluid ounces = 50 ml	
⅓ cup = 3 fluid ounces = 75 ml	
½ cup = 4 fluid ounces = 125 ml	
⅔ cup = 5 fluid ounces = 150 ml	
¾ cup = 6 fluid ounces = 175 ml	
1 cup = 8 fluid ounces = 250 ml	
2 cups = 1 pint = 500 ml	
1 quart = 1 litre	